Improv 2 Ideas

A new book of games and lists for the classroom and beyond

Compiled, Created and Invented by
Justine Jones and Mary Ann Kelley

MERIWETHER PUBLISHING LTD.
Colorado Springs, Colorado

Meriwether Publishing Ltd., Publisher
PO Box 7710
Colorado Springs, CO 80933-7710

Editor: Theodore O. Zapel
Assistant Editor: Nicole Deemes
Interior Design: Jan Melvin

© Copyright MMXIV Meriwether Publishing Ltd.
Printed in the United States of America
First Edition

Library of Congress Cataloging-in-Publication Data

Jones, Justine, 1949-
 Improv ideas 2 : a new book of games and lists for the classroom and
beyond / by Justine Jones and Mary Ann Kelley. -- First edition.
     pages cm
 Includes bibliographical references.
 ISBN 978-1-56608-195-5 (pbk.)
 1. Improvisation (Acting) 2. Games. I. Kelley, Mary Ann, 1948- II.
Title. III. Title: Improv ideas two.
 PN2071.I5J6815 2013
 792.02'8--dc23

                                        2013024505

        1   2   3   14   15   16

To the inspiration all around us!
— Justine Jones

To all of the young people who are growing because of drama in their lives;
To all of the teachers who use drama as a tool for life as well as a grade;
To all of the kids who were in my drama clases and have become such wonderful adults;
To my steadfast friends who have always been with me, giving me excitement, and peace, and courage;
To my favorite child and my favorite brother;
This book is yours with all my love and gratitude.
— MAK

Contents

Preface 1
Introduction 3

Warm-Ups 9

Adverb Game 11
Daily Activities 12
Adverbs 13

Archaeology Game 14
Artifacts 15

Who Invited You? 16
Bad Manners 17
Generic Scenes 18

Brand Name Game 19
Imaginary Brand Names 20

Don't Do That! 21
Commands 22

Museum of Oddities 23
Exhibitions and Collections 24

You Got Me What? 26
Gifts 27

Saying Hello 28
As If You Are 29

Hobbies 30
Real Hobbies 31

We're Going on a Vacation 32
Unusual and Imaginary Hobbies 33

Tableaux (Frozen Pictures) 34
Holidays 35

Backpack Game 36
Items in a Purse or Backpack 37

Let the Games Begin 38
Olympic Sports 39

I've Got the Message 40
Phone Calls 41

Preposition Game 42
Prepositions 43

And the Winner Is 44

Prizes for Best and Worst 45

Musical Comedy 46

Song Titles and Styles 47

My Pet Boa 48

Strange Pets 49

A Touch Of 50

Textures 51

Useful Utensils 52

Utensils 53

Why Can't I? 54

Whines 55

Characterization 57

Faculty Meeting 59

Academic Disciplines 60

What's Wrong with Me? 61

Annoying Medical Conditions 62

I'm an Ox! 63

Chinese Astrological Types 64

Clothes Make the Person 65

Clothing 66

Color Me Pink 68

Colors 69

Friends Forever 70

Friend Traits 71

High Five! 72

Gestures 73

My Tiara 74

Jewelry and Accessories 75

Please and Thank You 76

Manners 77

In the Mood 78

Moods 79

Phobia Game 80

Phobias 81

Relationship Dyads 84

Relationships 85

Skillful 86

Skills 87

Enclosed Spaces 88

Valley Girls vs. Snobs 89
  Stereotypes 90
It's My Name! 91
  Unusual Names 92
Job Interview 93
  Unusual Occupations 94
Devil Made Me Do It 95
  Vices 96
Virtuous Family 97
  Virtues 98
Trapped with a Libra 99
  Western Astrological Types 100

Narrative/Plot 101

Sherlock Holmes 103
  The Case of the ... .104
The Big Moment 105
  Climaxes 106
It's a Mystery 107
  Clue Sets 108
Our House 110
  Dwellings 111
Real Estate Agent 112
  Environments...113
Lima Beans 114
  Food 115
Glimpses 116
  Foreshadowing Situations 117
It's Your Lucky Day! 118
  Fortune Cookies 119
In the Manner Of ... .120
  Genres 121
It Happened Here 122
  Historical Events 123
The Birth of the Blobs 126
  Imaginary Bands 127
Two Thumbs Up! 128
  Imaginary Films 129
Resolutions 130
  New Year's Resolutions 131

A Bird in the Hand 132
   Common Sayings 133
Rituals...136
   Reasons to Celebrate 137
In the Lounge...138
   Rooms in a House 139
Read All about It..140
   Scrambled Headlines 141
   Real Headlines 143
Magic Shop 144
   Shops 145
Super Powers 146
   Super Skills 147
What If? 148
   Things You'd Like to See 149
Last Chance Saloon 150
   Unusual Town Names 151
Our Trip to Rio..152
   Vacation Destinations 153

The Answers at the Back of the Book...155
Animals of the Chinese Zodiac 157
Aligning Improv Games to the National Standards for Theatre Education 159
   Warm-Up Standards 161
   Characterization Standards 162
   Narrative/Plot Standards 163
Resources...164
About the Authors 167

Preface

Back in 2005 when *Improv Ideas: A Book of Games and Lists* was published, we were simply excited about sharing our ideas — ideas that had worked for us over many years of teaching drama. We knew that we both used improv in our classrooms, but we were not sure if others did. We knew that, traditionally, many drama teachers jump right into scripts, considering it more "serious" than improv, but we both had such good luck in engaging our students through this medium that we were excited to share.

Little did we know that many teachers were simply hungry for these ideas! We received numerous emails from beleaguered teachers who told us what *Improv Ideas* meant to them. Some shared with us their own ideas and techniques. Some of them used our ideas on index cards, and one even had a "Drama Cart" with card files of improv prompts.

This led us to write *Drama Games and Improvs: Games for the Classroom and Beyond.* It detailed a complete one-semester course based entirely on improv that Justine taught for twelve years. She developed it after twenty years of teaching a more traditional course based on script reading and sometimes writing. By having the emphasis on process rather than product (script and performance), we were doing something never done before as far as we knew — teaching drama concepts entirely through improvisation. (*Drama Games and Improvs* also contains successful games that do not require lists and are useable outside its curriculum, so it's worth a look.)

Again, we received many thank-you emails and positive reviews. Apparently, there were others out there who liked this concept. We were not teaching a class on improv per se but developing theatre concepts through improv games. This supported our belief that teaching through the process of games could not only develop theatre skills but involve students who had little interest in further studies in theatre. These students were not only introduced to theatre through fun and involving activities but also would develop communication skills and creativity.

What could be better than being able to think creatively on your feet?

Now we come to *Improv Ideas 2.* Why? Of course we have scoured the many theatre game books. Some of the games are wonderfully engaging and quite interesting. Some are even written in simple step-by-step language, not burdening the beginning teacher or director with lots of theory, which may be superfluous. But none of them included actual lists of ideas to go with the games. And so many of the games need lots of ideas.

Why do we provide lists to go with the games? We are aware that this might be seen by some as circumventing the creative process, but we have both taught for years and are well aware of time constraints, pupil reticence, and the fact that some of our colleagues, perhaps drafted into teaching drama because they have a degree in English, may not have extensive theatre backgrounds. And not only that. I remember well one summer afternoon when I had to ask the school custodians for ideas regarding crimes for our game of "CSI: Your Hometown." I had simply run out of things for which someone could be convicted! However, they had lots of ideas and relished sharing.

Many heads are better than one, of course. These ideas are incomplete. You, your students, and even your friends and family can happily add to them. If you live in a country other than the U.S., you will no doubt have different ideas than these U.S.-centric ideas. And if you are under forty, the same thing. Ideas are very time and place oriented. So go crazy and add your own! These are merely suggestions from our own lives to give you a start — not the final word.

Introduction

For your convenience, the following is a slightly adapted introduction from *Improv Ideas*. Things haven't changed that much in our game format, so please be aware that the same ideas apply. Our book structure is different, though. We have divided the book into three areas: warm-ups, characterization, and narrative/plot. This is new. In the past, all were included in one hodgepodge of alphabetized lists, and you could pick and choose based on your own interest or a chart in the back of the book. In the interest of being even more useful, we have done some of the work for you in advance. Maybe someday we will have an entire book devoted just to warm-ups. So enjoy. We're always interested in what you find useful and what other things we might include in the future that might help you even more. We are committed to providing ideas for drama game players, directors, and especially teachers — new or old, experienced in drama or not. We believe that improv is fun above all, and we hope you and your students will, too!

And Now Some Answers

What do you mean by improvisation?

When we talk about improvisation, improv, or impro, we mean the impromptu creation of a scene with lines and action extemporized as the scene progresses. Different directors for different groups allow varying degrees of preparation. TV's popular *Whose Line Is It Anyway?* demands on-the-spot performance from very experienced professionals. An elementary language arts teacher may spend a significant amount of time discussing plot and character elements with primary students before actual scenes are improvised. The improvisation may be performed before an understanding audience or before one director. It may be an end unto itself or the springboard of a finished product, such as those of The Second City's "Story Theatre."

How can I use improv?

For those new to improvisation, know that it can be used as an individual activity to fill time (sponges, in educational terms) or as an instructional method to teach students dramatic concepts or how to think creatively on their feet. As such, we feel that improv is not only fun but also invaluable. And our students think so, too.

We have found that keeping up a fast pace contributes to the effectiveness of the activity. Keith Johnstone always says, "Don't be prepared," and this is extremely important to emphasize, as beginning players tend to feel that more careful planning makes for better scenes. We always stress that improv is a process, not necessarily an end in itself. As such, participating is the key factor, not being clever. Also there is a fine line between judging an improv as a successful performance and critiquing the process. In general, when the group is new, it is very important to focus on the process rather than the product. Make certain that participants do not feel that they will be "graded" for anything other than doing their best. Improv must be both fun and non-threatening.

What is side coaching?

The side coaching section indicates how a leader might suggest improvements in the activity as it is going on. The action of the game does not stop or slow down for coaching, just as it would not slow down in a basketball game. Students soon get used to having and acting on that "little voice" in their ear as they perform.

Side coaching ideas may be followed by exclamation marks in the book but should be spoken in any way the director thinks appropriate.

Side coaching concepts may be introduced before playing improv games, or the director may just start side coaching. If players stop to listen, the director says, "Just keep on; listen to me, but don't look." "I'm like your conscience; listen to me and try to do what I say." "Keep going." Mary Ann is a fan of side coaching and uses it in improv and in rehearsals. Justine is not as enthusiastic and she uses it sparingly only if new improv-ers need help. Directors should use it — or not — as is comfortable for them.

What are the improv guidelines?

Regardless of the methods or goals of specific improvisations, there are a few guidelines that most improvisers use.

Just do it. Agree. Don't block. Improvisation depends upon teamwork and playing off one another. Refusing to play or changing the ideas is called blocking and does not carry the improv forward. Accept the first idea offered.

Have fun. Remember, improvs are a fun way to explore the abilities of one's self and fellow players, the group's dynamics, and of theatre. Follow the rules, follow the time limits, and share with your partners. Relax and have a good time. Improvs are not judged — participation is.

Keep it appropriate. Improv depends on everyone — participants and audience alike — having a good time without worrying about being offended or hurt. Therefore, there should be no profanity, obscenity, inappropriate references, hurtful statements, or cruelty. Everyone participating and observing should feel comfortable.

Did you make up all the games and lists?

Many of the games are Justine's original ideas. Others have come to us from sources long forgotten — the "Improv Grapevine," if you will. Others are classics we learned in college with no origin given. The lists came entirely from our own imaginations, the creativity of our students, and many hours with a dictionary and Wikipedia. We usually start an improv session with a player-generated list on the chalkboard.

We encourage you to add to the lists from your own creativity and that of your players.

Talking the Theatre Talk

Theatre Terms to Know (Including terms specific to this book)

Blocking (improv): Refusing to play, changing the idea offered, or any action in an improv that does not carry the improv forward.

Blocking (play production): The management of physical action in the playing space. The part of the stage used and why, the use of props and furniture, and the ways players move in the playing space are all part of blocking.

B-M-E: The basic plot elements of beginning-middle-end are abbreviated to B-M-E. (See the plot section on the next page.)

Conventions: The practices that make improvisations and theatrical productions successful for both actors and audience. Speaking loudly enough to be heard by fellow players and audience, facing the audience most of the time, and giving and taking focus are all conventions.

Climax: The moment of greatest dramatic intensity or the turning point in the action.

Crisis: A moment of high dramatic intensity or a turning point in the action, usually followed by a decrease in the suspense. (The final crisis is the climax.)

Denouement (day-noo-MAH): The unraveling of the plot, following the climax, in which the players show how and why everything turned out as it did. Unnecessary for many short improvs.

Director: Group leaders, teachers, or play directors. Players may also serve as directors for games.

Ensemble: A group constituting an organic whole or working together for a single effect.

Endowment: A player is "given" an attribute by others and has to discover and/or adapt to it.

Exposition: The background information that reveals "how it all began," specifically what happened prior to the time covered in the improv, what the characters are like, and what situation has arisen that will lead to a problem that must be resolved.

Focus: The person or thing that receives the attention of both the players and the audience. Focus shifts throughout the work.

Inciting incident (or episode): The introduction of a problem that changes the story forever. The point at which there is no turning back in the story; things will never be the same. This usually happens early in the work and drives the story.

Players: The participants in the improvs.

Playing space: The area in which the group performs. It may be a stage, raised platform, or part of a room.

Plot: The series of events or episodes that make up the action of the improv. (Includes exposition, inciting incident, rising action, climax, and denouement [optional].)

Rising action: The series of events, preceding the climax, which intensifies the conflict and, thereby, creates a feeling of suspense about the outcome.

Setting: The background time, place, weather, and circumstances in which the events in an improv take place.

Plot: a beginning, a middle, and an ending

Whether it is Shakespeare, *Saturday Night Live,* or your own improv, plot is important.

The **beginning** contains the *exposition* which establishes *who, where, when,* and *why.* Most improvisation requires that the information be delivered quickly and concisely. For improvs that start immediately, the first player must give as much information to fellow players as possible. The beginning ends with the *inciting incident* or introduction of the problem.

The **middle** contains the *rising action,* which is the action that leads up to a *crisis.* Longer improvs may have several crises each followed by a reduction in dramatic intensity, or *falling action,* which then leads into another increase in intensity and crisis.

The **ending** contains the final crisis — the moment of greatest dramatic intensity — which is called the *climax.* Improvs often end immediately after the climax. They may, however, offer the resolution and tying up of loose ends afforded with a *denouement.*

Groups: What, How, and When

Group Composition

How does one arrive at the groups for games? Changing group composition allows players to work with people they might not work with otherwise, but how do we get groups that are comfortable and work well together to change? Here are a few of our tricks:

Choose your own group: This technique is great with new players. It adds a level of comfort to the often uncomfortable or threatening idea of improvisation.

Work with a group that has one person you haven't worked with before: While allowing players to work with some people who are familiar, it allows them to expand their working relationships to include others in the large group.

Number off: Simple, but it works. Decide on the size of the groups you need. Divide the total number of players by the numbers of players in the group. Have players number off into the number of groups you need. Then all ones work together, all twos work together, etc. If there are remainders, have them work with a group of their choosing or your assignment.

Assign groups: Why not? Especially after the large group has worked for a while and you are familiar with the individual members' styles and abilities. This technique can lead to magic.

Group Size

Most of the games in this book are written to accommodate a large group of twenty-four to forty players. More than that and playing time with smaller groups becomes unwieldy; fewer than eighteen players and there often aren't enough to divide into larger groups. Groups (noted as "players" on the game pages) are as few as one and as many as six. These numbers are just suggestions. Individual directors may choose to use smaller or larger groups to accommodate their own large group and players' skills. Obviously, when these games are used to augment rehearsal, the numbers are based on the cast list.

Performance Order

"May we go first? Let us be first, oh, please!" We have discovered that deciding on performance order before the first improv leaves little room for anguish later. Volunteers eager to improv in front of the large group are music to any director's ears, but sorting through the volunteers can be as difficult as assigning reluctant players. Here are some tricks to try:

Volunteering: "Who wants to go first?" The first hand that pops up goes. "Next?" The next hand, and so forth. (Don't forget to write them down!)

Assigning: Alphabetically by last — or first — name of a group's representative. The first group to go was the last group in the previous improv.

Random: "Choose a number between one and twenty-five." Draw from facedown, numbered index cards or draw numbered ping-pong balls from a paper bag.

Combination of techniques.

Sample Games, Lists, and More Lists

Sample Games

At least one game is given for each list. Don't let it stop you from being inspired to make up your own game using a list.

Lists next to Games

Each list is printed on the page directly following the game with which the list is associated. Some games are easiest to play with a closely spaced list that only the director uses. The lists printed in the book are ideal for this application. For lists broken up for individuals or groups to draw, it's best to copy them onto cards or slips of paper.

Do Your Homework

Read and Cull

While we have used many of these games with all age groups, some of the games are not suitable for everyone. Even with suitable games, some of the words on the lists may not be right for all players. *You know your players.* Please read the game through for suitability in your particular situation. Check over the lists, too, for any words or concepts that might offend someone or lead to your players being offensive to others. It's easier to remove words from a list than to do damage control.

A chart at the beginning of each section will tell you at a glance how many players a game usually uses and whether the game requires equipment. It will also give information about preparation and playing times.

Guide to Visual References in This Book

(Found in the game page information bar.)

Uses

The games in *Improv Ideas 2* are broken into three primary uses: Warm-Up, Characterization, and Narrative/Plot. Each use is given its own section in the book, and those uses also head the info bar.

Budgeting Time for the Games

All of the times given are suggestions only. Directors should tailor the time requirements of the exercises to fit the group's needs.

Space Prep

Some games require configuring the playing space. This may be as simple as arranging chairs in a circle for the group or as complicated as creating a restaurant with three tables. The "Space Prep" box tells approximately how many minutes this activity will take.

Player Prep

Some of the games require players to start immediately (noted with a zero), others allow players to prepare. *Note:* Preparation does not mean rehearsal — just deciding who should play which role, how the scene should end, etc. We have found that the less prep time, the more spontaneous and effective the idea generation and comfort level. However, directors may choose to allow for more time depending on the group's comfort level. As the group becomes more proficient in improv, the prep time may decrease or even be dispensed with altogether.

Performance Time

Some games require a performance to be over within a certain amount of time; others are open-ended and allow the game to continue to its logical ending. Unless noted, timekeeping is casual and the games may end in *approximately* the time noted.

Players

This number indicates the optimum number of players for the game. Games may be played with more or fewer players as the size of the full group, the experience of the players, and the needs of the game dictate.

Equipment

The improv setting should have an assortment of simple chairs, stools, benches, and small tables (acting cubes optional) to bring into the acting area when needed. Specific equipment needed for each game is noted in the equipment box.

Difficulty

Each game in the "Warm-Ups" section has a difficulty rating: 1 is the easiest, 3 is the most difficult. The "Characterization" and "Narrative/Plot" sections do not have difficulty ratings included.

Teach and Practice Skills

Some of these games' teach and practice categories are exclusively for drama teachers, but many games speak to universal group attributes such as concentration, creativity, group dynamics, listening and silence, non-vocal communication, observation, and spontaneity. Skills that are taught and practiced in the game are in black.

Blocking and Conventions: Use of stage areas and the conventions of theatre (speaking loudly, facing the audience, etc.) are stressed in these games.

Characterization: While one entire section of this book is devoted to characterization, many games with other focus points also depend on characterization. Just think of it as a bonus!

Concentration: Paying close attention to the task at hand and to fellow players is required in these games.

Creativity: Thinking in unusual and even personally risky ways is encouraged in these games. The reward is acceptance and appreciation of each player's work.

Ensemble Acting: The give-and-take and consideration for the individuals in the group, as well as the group's effort, are important in these games.

Group Dynamics: These games have no stars. Players must work together to make everything come out right. Waiting one's turn is often very important.

Listening and Silence: Attentive listening is important. Quietly waiting and appreciating the work of others is essential.

Non-Vocal Communication: Body language and gesture are often as important as what is said. These games encourage the use and observation of players' non-spoken work.

Observation: What players see, what they have seen, and how they use observation are the keys to success for these games.

Physical Control: Precise movement and physical accuracy are important in making these games effective.

Plot Structure: Beginnings, middles, and endings that work are what make these games successful. A complete story in the allotted time is the goal. The final section of this book is devoted to creation of narrative or plot. Many of the other games also emphasize narrative.

Spontaneity: Thinking and acting quickly is the goal of these games. From just fair to wonderful, it's the in-the-moment work that counts.

Warm-Ups

Warm-ups, sometimes known as icebreakers, do just what the name implies: they warm up individuals and groups to further drama activities. As such, they are usually short in duration and encourage "in the moment" spontaneity, quick thinking on one's feet, and — quite often — thinking outside the box. It is important to note, however, that they are not necessarily "easy" activities, and sometimes require prior experience in improv for participants to feel comfortable. (A slow progression in warm-ups to more extended and focused improv work is detailed in *Drama Games and Improvs.*) For this reason we have rated them one through three in terms of complexity, with one being the easiest. Since you know your group, you are the best judge of how to use these, of course.

In general, warm-ups involving the entire group are usually much less threatening than those in small groups, pairs, or individuals, but this is not always the case. Again, you know best! Please note that more than one list can be used for the same activity

Warm-Ups at a Glance

Game	Page	Space Prep	Player Prep	Performance	Group Size	Difficulty	Blocking and Conventions	Characterization	Concentration	Creativity	Ensemble Acting	Group Dynamics	Listening and Silence	Non-Vocal Communication	Observation	Physical Control	Plot Structure	Spontaneity	Equipment
Adverb Game	11	0	0	5	all	1		●		●				●		●		●	
Archaeology Game	14	0	0	3-5	2	2					●	●		●	●	●		●	
Who Invited You?	16	0	0	5	3	3		●		●	●			●	●	●		●	
Brand Name Game	19	0	5-10	3-5	2	3		●		●	●		●	●			●	●	
Don't Do That!	21	0	0	3-5	2	2		●		●	●			●			●	●	
Museum of Oddities	23	0	0	5	1+	3				●								●	
You Got Me What?	26	0	0	5-7	4	2				●		●			●			●	
Saying Hello	28	0	0	5-10	2+	1				●		●			●			●	
Hobbies	30	0	0	5	all	1			●	●				●		●		●	
We're Going on a Vacation	32	0	0	3-5	2	3				●	●				●			●	
Tableaux (Frozen Pictures)	34	0	0-2	5-7	3-5	2	●	●		●	●	●		●		●			
Backpack Game	36	0	3	5	3	3		●		●	●						●	●	opt.
Let the Games Begin	38	0	0	3-5	2	2		●	●	●	●		●	●	●	●		●	
I've Got the Message	40	0	0	3-5	1	3				●				●				●	
Preposition Game	42	0	0	1	2	2				●				●		●		●	
And the Winner Is…	44	0	0	5	4	2		●		●	●			●				●	
Musical Comedy	46	0	5	5	3-5	3				●	●	●		●				●	
My Pet Boa	48	0	0	5	2	2				●	●			●	●	●		●	
A Touch Of …	50	0	0	5	all	1			●	●				●				●	●
Useful Utensils	52	0	0	5	all	1				●				●		●		●	●
Why Can't I?	54	0	0	3-5	2	2		●		●								●	

Adverb Game

Directions

- The group spreads out across the room.
- The director suggests an everyday activity, then calls out an adverb.
- All players individually perform the activity in the manner of the suggested adverb simultaneously.
- At the director's discretion, adverbs may be changed (frequently), and activities may be changed (less frequently).

Examples

- Waking up — angrily, calmly, elegantly.
- Writing a letter — carelessly, bravely, doubtfully.
- Ordering in a restaurant — frantically, irritably, thoughtfully.

Side Coaching

- Make sure you show movement.
- Use your body as well as your face.
- Use more than one of the five senses.

Evaluation/Critique

- Which adverbs lent themselves to broad movement?
- Which adverbs seemed to suggest more refined movement?
- Which adverbs were difficult to match to the activity? Why?

Challenges and Refinements

- Divide into pairs for the exercise.
- Choose one activity and an adverb to suggest a scene, either in mime or vocalized.

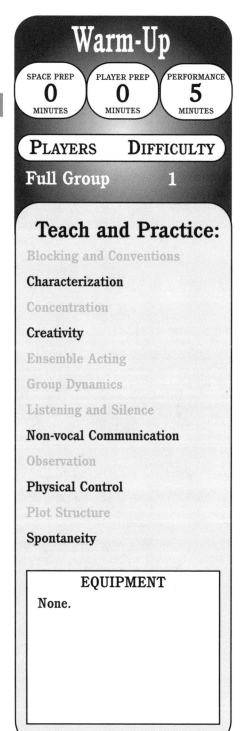

Warm-Up

SPACE PREP	PLAYER PREP	PERFORMANCE
0	0	5
MINUTES	MINUTES	MINUTES

PLAYERS	DIFFICULTY
Full Group	1

Teach and Practice:

Blocking and Conventions
Characterization
Concentration
Creativity
Ensemble Acting
Group Dynamics
Listening and Silence
Non-vocal Communication
Observation
Physical Control
Plot Structure
Spontaneity

EQUIPMENT
None.

Daily Activities

applying scent/perfume/cologne

brushing your teeth

combing your hair

drawing

drinking coffee

driving to work/school

eating a messy sandwich

eating breakfast

fixing a meal

getting dressed

going to bed

listening to music

loading a dishwasher

looking for a dropped contact lens

looking for a lost object

mixing a cake

ordering in a restaurant

picking up broken dishes

putting in a contact lens

putting on earrings/jewelry

putting on makeup

putting the dishes away

reading a book

reading a letter

sharpening a pencil

shopping for new clothes

sweeping the floor

taking a bath

taking a nap

taking a shower

taking a walk

taking an exam

taking medicine

talking on the phone

thinking up an excuse for being late

trying to get into clothes that are too small

trying to put on a seat belt

trying to start the car

vacuuming

waiting for the bus

waiting for the doctor/dentist

waking up

walking the dog

washing the dishes

washing the dog/cat

watching a movie

watching TV

working at the computer

working out

writing a letter

writing a poem

Adverbs

abnormally
abrasively
acerbically
acrobatically
adventurously
affably
affirmingly
aggressively
aimlessly
angrily
anxiously
apathetically
arrogantly
awkwardly
blindly
boisterously
boldly
bravely
brightly
briskly
brutally
busily
calculatingly
calmly
captivatingly
carefully
carelessly
cattily
cautiously
cheerfully
chillingly
circumspectly
classily
cleverly
coltishly

compellingly
confidently
coolly
courageously
curiously
daringly
defiantly
deliberately
demurely
directly
doubtfully
dreamily
dynamically
eagerly
easily
effortlessly
elegantly
energetically
enthusiastically
expressively
exuberantly
falteringly
feebly
feverishly
fiercely
forcefully
frantically
furiously
furtively
gently
girlishly
gracefully
graciously
haggardly
happily

hastily
haughtily
heedlessly
hysterically
icily
impatiently
inattentively
inductively
innocently
inquisitively
intensely
irritably
jauntily
joyously
jumpily
laboriously
laboredly
lazily
lightly
limply
loudly
meanderingly
merrily
mysteriously
nervously
nimbly
noisily
nonchalantly
oafishly
obediently
obnoxiously
oddly
painfully
placidly
politely

promptly
provocatively
purposefully
quaintly
quickly
quietly
quirkily
quixotically
randomly
rapidly
recklessly
relaxed
reluctantly
roughly
rudely
sadly
shakily
shyly
silently
sleepily
slowly
smoothly
softly
solemnly
sorrowfully
speedily
spiritedly
spritely
stealthily
sternly
straightforwardly
stylishly
suddenly
suspiciously
swaggeringly

swiftly
tenderly
tensely
testily
thoughtfully
torturously
triumphantly
twitchily
unabashedly
unevenly
unresponsively
urgently
victoriously
violently
vivaciously
waggishly
weakly
wearily
wildly
wistfully
wobbly
wolfishly
worriedly
yearningly
youthfully
zealously
zestfully

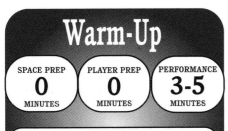

Warm-Up

SPACE PREP	PLAYER PREP	PERFORMANCE
0 MINUTES	**0** MINUTES	**3-5** MINUTES

PLAYERS	DIFFICULTY
2	2

Teach and Practice:

Blocking and Conventions

Characterization

Concentration

Creativity

Ensemble Acting

Group Dynamics

Listening and Silence

Non-vocal Communication

Observation

Physical Control

Plot Structure

Spontaneity

EQUIPMENT
None.

Archaeology Game

Directions

- Divide the group into pairs.
- The players are all anthropologists/archaeologists in the year 3500.
- Each pair receives the name of an object representing an artifact they have dug up in the ruins of (the current year) in (current place). The archaeologists want this object to be included in a new exhibition. The artifact is unfamiliar and not in use in 3500, so a function must be inferred.

Examples

- The object is an earring. In 3500, there is no such thing as personal adornment, so these scientists decide that it is a form of currency.
- The object is a bell. Loud noises are forbidden in this future world, so the scientists decide that 2013 was a year of reckless crime and that the bell was a means of torture.

Side Coaching

- Focus on the physical properties of your object.
- If you didn't know what this was, what might you think it is?
- Be open to everybody's ideas before your choose.
- Why doesn't your culture know what this is?

Evaluation/Critique

- Did each scientist provide a unique explanation or development for the use of the object?
- Did they persuade you that this object is important enough to get into the museum?
- Did they give you an inkling of why this object might be so unfamiliar to a future world?

The hit musical *We Will Rock You* based on the music of Queen is a similar situation about a future generation's understanding of 20th Century rock music where Britney Spears is the "biggest, baddest musician of them all."

action figure
baby bottle
Barbie doll
baton
blow dryer
book
candlestick
candy bar
chopsticks
Christmas ornaments
cigarette lighter
cigarettes
clown nose
computer, desktop
cuff links
curling iron
deck of cards
dog collar
dog leash
doll house
duct tape
DVD or CD
extension cord
face mask/sleep mask
fingernail clippers
Frisbee
Game Boy
garlic press
golf club
greeting cards
hair dryer
hair roller
hat
highlighter
hose
jacks
key
key ring
kite
lipstick

lunch box
marbles
match book
microphone
mobile phone
motorcycle helmet
pacifier
pen
pill box
Play-Doh
pocket watch
postcard
potato masher
Q-tip, cotton swab
roll of toilet tissue
rolling pin
rubber ball
rubber band
rubber chicken
rubber duckie
scarf
scissors
shovel or spade
Slinky
slippers
snuff box
steno pad
straw
sunglasses
tape
teddy bear
tie
tie tack
top
toy boat
umbrella
whoopee cushion
wrapping paper
wrench
yardstick

SPACE PREP	PLAYER PREP	PERFORMANCE
0	0	5
MINUTES	MINUTES	MINUTES

PLAYERS	DIFFICULTY
3	3

Teach and Practice:

Blocking and Conventions

Characterization

Concentration

Creativity

Ensemble Acting

Group Dynamics

Listening and Silence

Non-vocal Communication

Observation

Physical Control

Plot Structure

Spontaneity

EQUIPMENT
None.

Who Invited You?

Directions
- Divide the players into groups of three.
- The groups are participating in a generic scene.
- Each of the three has a "bad manners" card.
- During the course of the scene, each player uses the bad manners at least twice.
- When the others guess what the bad behavior is, they react appropriately.

Example
The bad manners are Player 1 eating with mouth open, Player 2 picking nose, and Player 3 speaking over others. The scene drawn is a birthday party. It starts with the cake being served. Player 1 starts to eat eagerly, talking with her mouth open. This annoys Player 3 who tries to stop Player 1 by talking over her. Player 2 is busily picking his nose, and the other two suddenly turn on him. Player 1 accidentally spits out food as she chews. Player 2 talks with his finger still up his nose. Player 3 escalates the talking over the others to show how disgusted she is. Player 2 is flummoxed, not knowing what has set them off. He pretends to swallow a booger and the others leave, disgusted.

Side Coaching
- Don't forget to listen to and watch your fellow actors during the scene.
- You have at least two chances to show your bad manners, you don't have to get it all in at once.
- Remember to respond to the bad manners as you see them. Even while you are guessing what they are, they should be obvious.

Evaluation/Critique
- Was each bad habit incorporated into the scene?
- Did each bad habit have physical, vocal, and emotional components?
- Did each bad habit suggest a certain type of personality/character?

allowing your children to misbehave in public

always asking for money/not paying your part

always talking about yourself or steering conversation to yourself

bad personal hygiene

begging for attention

being annoyed all the time

being overly critical

blaming others for your mistakes/not admitting you're wrong

blowing your nose loudly in public

borrowing and not returning things

bullying

burping

chewing gum with your mouth open

chewing on hair

clicking your tongue with disapproval

constantly complaining or whining

coughing and not covering your mouth

cutting in line

discounting others' opinions

dropping gum on the sidewalk

eating with your mouth open

gossiping

hogging/dominating the conversation

honking

ignoring others

interrupting conversations

inviting yourself along when not invited

keeping a disdainful look on your face

listening to loud music in public

littering

making disapproving faces and sounds

making everyone in a group conform to your needs

making loud noises while eating

never volunteering to help out

not giving a seat to someone in need

not picking up your mess

not saying "excuse me"

not saying "please" and "thank you"

not saying "sorry" when bumping into someone

picking one's nose

pushing or shoving

pushing into conversations

pushing/shoving in public

putting others down

saying "yes but" to most everything

sending abusive emails or texts

sending texts while at a meal

slurping drinks

speaking over someone

speaking too loudly/shouting

spitting

standing in the middle of the sidewalk

standing someone up

taking a baby to a formal event

taking up two parking spaces/stealing a parking space

talking during a film

talking on the phone loudly in public

telling stupid jokes/punning all the time

throwing garbage/trash on the ground

trying to be the center of attention

using bleeped-out swear words constantly

walking down the street *en masse*

wearing inappropriate clothing

Generic Scenes

attending a baby shower

attending a wedding

attending a wedding shower

becoming engaged

being granted a patent for your invention

celebrating a birthday

celebrating a special anniversary

celebrating your candidate winning an election

escaping from a mugger

first dance

first date

first day of school

first day on the job

first kiss

first pet

first time you baked a cake

first time you drove a car

first time you met a celebrity

first time you opened your eyes after surgery

getting a grant funded

getting a promotion

getting admitted to college

getting an A on a test

getting divorced

getting married

giving a eulogy at a funeral

going to your first prom

graduating from high school

having a baby

having your book published

kindergarten graduation

landing your first job

meeting your significant other's parents for the first time

meeting your soul mate

popping the question

qualifying for a school team

qualifying for the Olympics

retiring

time you almost died

time you baked your thousandth cake

time you bought a car

time you bought a house

time you caught a robber

time you flew in an airplane

time you flunked your driver's test … for the third time

time you got sick on a ride

time you had a surprise party

time you left home

time you lost your contact lens

time you lost your paycheck

time you met the love of your life

time you rode a camel

time you rode a roller coaster

time you saw a crime being committed

time you went to Disneyland/Disney World

time you won an award

time you won the lottery

time your dog really did eat your homework

toasting at a wedding

winning an award

winning the lottery

Brand Name Game

Directions

- Director leads discussion of interview techniques using who, what, when, where, why, and how (Five Ws and an H).
- Director leads discussion of how people interviewed need to respond knowledgeably, enthusiastically, and to the point.
- Director divides players into pairs.
- Each pair gets a brand name for a product. (The director may choose whether or not to tell both players what the product is.)
- One person in the pair is a newspaper business reporter, and the other is the new product publicist for the manufacturer.
- The reporter interviews the publicist about the qualities and properties of this new item.
- The publicist tries to make the product sound riveting, new, and highly desirable.

Examples

- The product is a magazine called *The Fool.* The reporter tries to understand the choice of the title; the publicist tells about a wide range of foolish activities included in the magazine, going into detail about one or two.
- The product is a car called *Poseidon.* The reporter tries to understand the choice of the name, and the publicist explains that the car is actually a submarine.

Side Coaching

- To the interviewer — Use interview techniques. The five Ws and H.
- To the interviewee — Be confident. Really sell your product.
- To the interviewee — Don't be afraid to go out on a limb. Make up properties that seem likely. The sky's the limit.

Evaluation/Critique

- Did the explanations fit the name?
- Were the interviewer's questions designed to elicit more than simple yes or no answers? (Open-ended questions?)
- Did the interviewee make the product sound interesting? Did he or she create a picture in your mind?

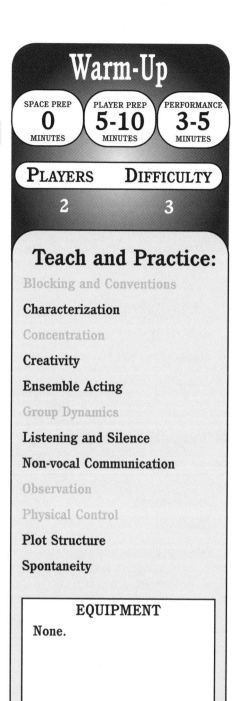

Warm-Up

SPACE PREP	PLAYER PREP	PERFORMANCE
0 MINUTES	5-10 MINUTES	3-5 MINUTES

PLAYERS	DIFFICULTY
2	3

Teach and Practice:

Blocking and Conventions

Characterization

Concentration

Creativity

Ensemble Acting

Group Dynamics

Listening and Silence

Non-vocal Communication

Observation

Physical Control

Plot Structure

Spontaneity

EQUIPMENT
None.

Imaginary Brand Names

Cars

Alpine

Bronco

Croydon

Derby

Dionysus

Exotic

Faraway

Gazelle

Hermes

Kenilworth

Kensington

Kent

Komodo

Lighthouse

Lockout

Neptune

Nessie

Nordic

Orienteer

Pan

Pluto

Pony

Poseidon

Quest

Racer

Silverback

Sprint

Stallion

Superb

Supremo

Traveler

Underwear

Bondage

Cassandra

Flaviols

Gianni's

Lasso

Leonardo's

Leonora

Leopard

Venus

Whiplash

Magazines

5000 BC

Awesomeness

Brave New World

Colors

Crackle

Digitize Me!

Dude

Dudettes

Dynamite

Easy Listenin'

Fool, The

Homebody

Jobless Journal

Layabout

Layback

Loosen Up

Mama's

Monster Mash

Numbers

Owl, The

Papa's

Punster

SHOUT!

Sparkle

Tax Evaders Digest

Trickster, The

Valley Girls

Way Out

Wicked

Word!

Zombie

Cereal

Barbie

Bumpers

Sugar Snaps

Skater Snaps

Don't Do That!

Directions

- In pairs, players go to the front of the room. Each person is given three commands on individual cards.
- The audience chooses a scene such as a first date, the first day of school, etc. (Use the list of "Generic Scenes" on page 18 or in *Improv Ideas* on page 159.
- The players perform a scene integrating their commands in a logical and motivated way.
- Other dialogue may or may not be used.

Example

Player A gets "Go away," "Just do it," and "Stop that." Player B gets "Be careful," "Go slowly," and "Cover your eyes." The scene is a swimming lesson. Player A stands at the side of the pool, embarrassed because he is afraid, telling those around to "Go away!" Player B comes up and tells him to "Be careful!" Player A tells himself to "Just do it!" Player B tells him to "Go slowly," trying to be encouraging while pushing Player A towards the water. Player A gets angry and tells Player B to "Stop that!" Player A then ignores Player B's advice to "Cover your eyes!"

Side Coaching

- Let your commands drive the actions.
- Don't forget the parameters of the scene. Stay in the place and activity.
- Ask yourself why you are saying that command. That will help you know how to say it.

Evaluation/Critique

- Were the commands integrated into the scene?
- Did they make sense?
- Did the commands carry the scene forward?
- Did the scene come to a logical conclusion?
- If other dialogue was used, did the commands fit in seamlessly, or were they jarring and random?

Challenges and Refinements

- If other dialogue was used, try doing the scenes using commands only.
- If only the commands were used, try the scenes with additional dialogue.
- Use the commands in any order and as often as you like.

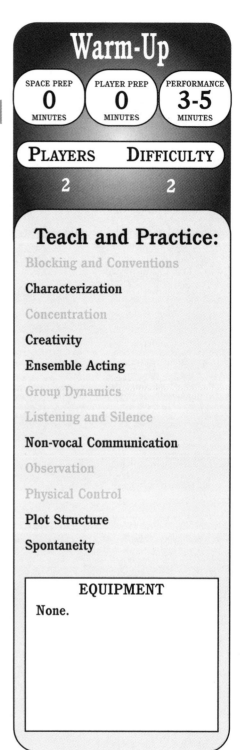

Warm-Up

SPACE PREP	PLAYER PREP	PERFORMANCE
0 MINUTES	0 MINUTES	3-5 MINUTES

PLAYERS	DIFFICULTY
2	2

Teach and Practice:

Blocking and Conventions

Characterization

Concentration

Creativity

Ensemble Acting

Group Dynamics

Listening and Silence

Non-vocal Communication

Observation

Physical Control

Plot Structure

Spontaneity

EQUIPMENT
None.

Commands

Ask me again!

Avert your gaze!

Be back soon!

Be careful!

Beg!

Behave!

Beware!

Bring it here now!

Bug off!

Catch me!

Cease!

Come back!

Come here!

Cover your eyes!

Desist!

Do it!

Do it later!

Do it now!

Don't act like a baby!

Don't be a sissy!

Don't be rude!

Don't be scared!

Don't do that!

Don't forget!

Don't go in there!

Don't go there!

Don't, I beg you!

Don't interrupt me!

Don't leave me!

Don't listen!

Don't litter!

Don't look!

Don't look at me
 like that!

Don't look back!

Don't look down!

Don't look up!

Don't mess with me!

Don't sass back!

Don't stop yet!

Don't talk!

Don't talk to me!

Don't talk to me
 like that!

Don't touch me!

Don't touch that!

Don't watch!

Don't you dare do that!

Drink this!

Duck!

Eat your food!

Feel better!

Forget it!

Freeze!

Get away!

Get cleaned up!

Get down!

Get lost!

Get out of here!

Give it back!

Give me that!

Go away!

Go get it now!

Go in there now!

Go on now!

Go slowly!

Go to bed!

Heads up!

I want one now!

Just do it!

Keep your eye on
 the ball!

Leave!

Leave me!

Leave me alone!

Let it go!

Let me see!

Let's go now!

Look!

Look alive!

Look at this!

Look out!

Lose the frown/
 smile/etc.

Make my day!

Mind your manners!

No more!

Please!

Remember that!

Say cheese!

Scram!

See you later!

See you soon!

Shhhh!

Shut up!

Sit down!

Sit still!

Slow down!

Stand up!

Stay away!

Stay back!

Stop!

Stop crying!

Stop fidgeting!

Stop it!

Stop laughing!

Stop looking!

Stop swearing!

Stop talking!

Stop that racket!

Take care!

Take that!

Take that off!

Tell me now!

That's enough now!

Watch me!

Watch out!

Watch the birdie!

Watch this!

Watch this spot!

Watch your feet!

Watch your step!

Watch yourself!

Museum of Oddities

Directions

- The director chooses a "curator."
- The curator draws a card that tells what he or she curates.
- The curator then introduces the group to the exhibition without telling them directly what it is.
- The audience may guess the type of collection through deduction and open questioning but not direct questions such as, "Is it _____?"
- The game ends when the audience has guessed what this exhibition is.

Example

The Museum of Board Games. The curator excitedly has the group think back to their cherished childhood memories. She reminds them of the characters, the colors, the conflict. A player might say, "But I don't remember riding one like this." The curator would reply, "Of course no one actually rode one, most people just sat on the floor or around a table." Another player might say, "I remember the dealer always cheating." The curator would say, "Most of the time you probably got to choose your own game pieces, didn't you?" Another player would say, "Imagine, having a museum for Monopoly." And the curator would say, "Not just Monopoly, we have Chutes and Ladders over here, and Candy Land over here." A final player would say, "I think it's great having a museum for all of the board games." The curator would say, "It's a great pleasure to have a group such as yours visiting, the Museum of Board Games. Let me direct your attention over here … "

Side Coaching

- Show us the amazing variety in this collection!
- Explain why this is unique in the entire world.

Evaluation/Critique

- Did the curator lead you in the right direction by explaining facets of the collection without giving you the answer?
- Did the group's questions narrow the curator's hints or go off on tangents?

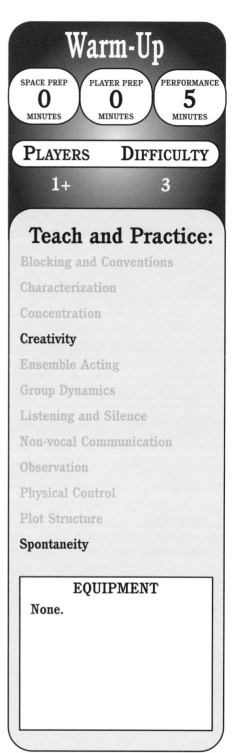

Warm-Up

SPACE PREP	PLAYER PREP	PERFORMANCE
0 MINUTES	0 MINUTES	5 MINUTES

PLAYERS	DIFFICULTY
1+	3

Teach and Practice:

Blocking and Conventions

Characterization

Concentration

Creativity

Ensemble Acting

Group Dynamics

Listening and Silence

Non-vocal Communication

Observation

Physical Control

Plot Structure

Spontaneity

EQUIPMENT
None.

Exhibitions and Collections

action figures

antique cars

antique pewter

antique silver

art

art glass

athletic memorabilia

ball caps

balls

Barbie dolls

baseball cards

baseballs

baskets

batik material

beads

Beanie Babies

bells

belt buckles

blocks

board games

bobble heads

bonsai plants

book covers

bottles

brands

buttons

Cabbage Patch Kids dolls

candles

candle holders

candlesticks

card games

carnival glass

cartoon strips

CDs

cereal boxes

children's books

Christmas villages

clocks

coins

colors of dirt/sand

comic books

concert posters

cookie jars

costumes

cuff links

cut glass

depression glass

dice

die casts

Disney character memorabilia

dog collars

doll houses

dream catchers

DVDs

earrings

eating utensils

Elvis paintings on velvet

family trees

figurines

film posters

film stills

fingernail polish

first editions of books

flags

footballs

fossils

gemstones

golf clubs

guns

hats

Hummel figurines

insulators

jewelry

kachina dolls

kaleidoscopes

kites

knives

Legos

light bulbs

lipstick

lunch boxes

Exhibitions and Collections

magazines

magnets

mandalas

marbles

masks

matchbooks

matryoshka dolls

military memorabilia

minerals

miniatures

model cars

model railroads

model trains

movie props

movie star autographs

music boxes

musical instruments

Navajo blankets

netsuke

old photographs

old toys

ornaments

paper money

pens

perfume bottles

perfumes

pins

plates

pool balls

postcards

pot holders

pottery

presidential autographs

puppets

purses

quilts

recipes

ribbons

rocks

rope

shells

shoes

skateboards

Smurfs

snapshots

snow globes

snuff boxes

spoons

stamps

stones

storyteller pottery

stuffed animals

surfboards

tarot cards

tattoo designs

taxidermy

tea cozies

teapots

teddy bears

theatre programs

thimbles

ties

tiles

Toby mugs

tops

torture equipment

trading cards

types of wood

umbrellas

underwear

vintage clothing

vinyl records

walking sticks

wooden toys

yarn

Zuni fetishes

Warm-Up

SPACE PREP	PLAYER PREP	PERFORMANCE
0	0	5-7
MINUTES	MINUTES	MINUTES

PLAYERS	DIFFICULTY
4	2

Teach and Practice:

Blocking and Conventions

Characterization

Concentration

Creativity

Ensemble Acting

Group Dynamics

Listening and Silence

Non-vocal Communication

Observation

Physical Control

Plot Structure

Spontaneity

EQUIPMENT
None.

You Got Me What?

Directions

- Divide into groups of four.
- One member is selected to be the birthday boy/girl.
- The others in the group each receive the name of a gift (real or imaginary) on a card.
- Sitting in a circle, they each present their "gifts" to the birthday person who does not know what the gift is.
- It is the gift giver's job to give the birthday boy or girl enough information so that he or she is able to guess the gift.
- The recipient then has to react to that gift in a logical manner.

Examples

- The gift is an iPad. The giver hints, "I hope you don't already have one. I know most people do." "I figured you could use it in school." "I really enjoy Angry Birds." "I know you like FaceTime."
- The gift is a toboggan. The giver provides hints such as, "Well, it snowed a lot this year!" I had one when I was a kid. It was really fast." "I know it's flat around here, but you can still have fun!"

Side Coaching

- Listen carefully to hints the giver provides you.
- Use the giver's physical as well as verbal hints to understand your gift.

Evaluation/Critique

- Were the clues logical? Easy to guess? Too obvious?
- What made for interesting clues?
- Did the recipient react differently to different gifts? Were the reactions plausible?

Challenges and Refinements

- Give imaginary gifts.
- Have the entire group (of four) react to these gifts once they're guessed.
- Develop the gift into a scene; for example, everyone gets excited about the toboggan, and all book a trip to the mountains to use it.

animal

beautiful rock from a beach

book of poetry

bouquet of flowers

box of special candy

breakfast in bed

chauffeur for a day

chef for a day

compilation of memoirs

crystal ball

dog collar

essential massage oils

famed print/lithograph

favorite lost toy

first edition of a book

fortune cookies

fossil

found item from a charity shop (thrift store)

garden tools/seeds

gourmet ice cream

handmade tile/jewelry

homemade book of recipes

homemade cookies

homemade cupcakes

homemade greeting cards

homemade jam

items from a foreign country

kite

lace

massager

menu from a restaurant, then a trip there

music compilations

neck rest

note cards from a museum shop

old memories on a DVD

original story/song

photo album of special photos

photo locket

picnic basket of food

pinhole camera

placemats

pocket watch

Polaroid camera

quilt of memories/photos

ribbons

scarf

scented pen

sea shells

servant for a day

singing telegram

something nostalgic

something totally unexpected

spices for included recipes

surprise trip to zoo/circus

"this is your life" interview on DVD

tool kit

treasure box

tree to plant

trip to an astrologer/palm reader/fortune
    teller

unique scarf/hat

vintage clothing

yarn

Warm-Up

SPACE PREP	PLAYER PREP	PERFORMANCE
0 MINUTES	**0** MINUTES	**5-10** MINUTES

PLAYERS	DIFFICULTY
2+	1

Teach and Practice:

Blocking and Conventions

Characterization

Concentration

Creativity

Ensemble Acting

Group Dynamics

Listening and Silence

Non-vocal Communication

Observation

Physical Control

Plot Structure

Spontaneity

EQUIPMENT
None.

Saying Hello

Directions
- Entire group stands or sits in a circle and numbers off.
- Odd-numbered participants get a "Hello" suggestion. Even-numbered players get an "I'm Fine" suggestion.
- Starting with number one, start a conversation using the suggestion on the card.
- Number two answers with his card suggestion and the scenarios continue.
- Group titles the scenario.
- Group decides what happens next.

Examples
- One's card reads, "Say 'Hello' as if you are thrilled to see them" and two's reads, "Say 'I'm Fine' as if you are unsure of who the other person is." The scene is titled by the group "Mistaken Identity." The group then decides that the first person wants try to pursue the second, while the second, after several aborted attempts, has to reveal that he has no idea who number one is.
- One's card reads, "Say 'Hello' as if you are afraid." Two's card says, "Say 'I'm Fine' as if you are not fine at all." The group titles this "At the Hospital" and suggests that one is terrified of infection and two is unable to allay his fears because he knows one really does have an infection.

Evaluation/Critique
- Was the title illustrative of the suggested scene?
- Did vocal tones convey meanings?
- Did physical demeanor convey meanings?
- Could this develop into an interesting scene from the ideas put forth?

Challenges and Refinements
- Have the group choose a pair to act out a suggested scene.
- Allow other group members to enter the scene.
- Suggest other possible dialogue conversations.

Discussion
- How are these scenarios enacted daily?
- Ask participants to note one to bring to the group the next session.

As If You Are ...

Say "Hello" as if you are ...

afraid.

angry.

apprehensive.

being forced to be nice.

being really phony.

better than they are.

bored.

confused.

cool and they're not.

disgusted.

forced to say it.

glad to see the person.

happy to be alive.

in a hurry.

inferior.

just being polite.

meeting someone important.

not a speaker of their language.

not sure what to say.

on auto pilot.

reluctant to say it.

resigned.

sad.

superior.

suspicious.

speaking a language they don't understand.

thrilled to see them.

wanting to get out of there.

wondering who they are.

Say "I'm Fine" as if you are ...

afraid.

angry and they should know it.

angry at being spoken to.

automatically responding.

being obedient.

confused.

disgusted.

forced to talk to them.

heartbroken.

in a hurry.

in awe of the person.

inferior.

not a speaker of the language.

not fine at all.

not happy to be alive.

not knowing the person.

not liking the other person.

not sure how you are.

not wanting to tell them.

smelling something bad.

speaking to a person who was once your boss.

superior.

unsure of what to say.

unsure of who the other person is.

wanting to be left alone.

wanting to get away.

wishing they hadn't asked.

wondering why they're acting so strangely.

SPACE PREP	PLAYER PREP	PERFORMANCE
0	0	5
MINUTES	MINUTES	MINUTES

PLAYERS	DIFFICULTY
Full Group	1

Teach and Practice:

Blocking and Conventions

Characterization

Concentration

Creativity

Ensemble Acting

Group Dynamics

Listening and Silence

Non-vocal Communication

Observation

Physical Control

Plot Structure

Spontaneity

EQUIPMENT
None.

Hobbies

Directions
- The group spreads out in the room. Players find their own spaces.
- In ten- to fifteen-second intervals, the director calls out a hobby.
- Each player silently enacts being involved with this hobby.
- At appropriate moments, the director stops the group to watch particularly interesting enactments.
- Group titles the scenario.
- Play continues for approximately five minutes.

Side Coaching
- It's OK to pantomime specific objects in the enactment.
- Make your movements precise and specific.
- Add variety; don't just repeat the same action.
- Show different aspects of the hobby.

Evaluation/Critique
- Which hobby did you find the easiest or most difficult to portray without physical props?
- What aspects of the hobby made it easier to enact? Were some more abstract than others? Did some need another person to make it work for you?

attending sporting events

baseball/soccer, etc.

bonsai

cards

causing trouble

church

clubbing

collecting
(see list of collections on page 24)

computer games

cooking

crafts

cycling

dancing

dating

dining out

DIY

dog training

doll houses

doodling

drinking

entertaining

exercising

exploring

Facebook

flower arranging

flying

gardening

genealogy

going to amusement parks

going to concerts

going to the movies

going to plays

going to restaurants

gymnastics

hang gliding

hiking

ice skating

improvising

inventing things

juggling

karaoke

kite flying

knitting

listening to music

listening to the radio

making ceramics

making lists

making model rockets

making pottery

making ships in bottles

martial arts

model trains

orienteering

painting

pets

photography

pinball machines

playing an instrument

playing golf

playing in a band

playing pool

practicing scales

reading books

reading poetry

riding

running/jogging

sailing

scrapbooking

scuba diving

shopping

skateboarding

skiing

sledding

sleeping

snorkeling

snowboarding

surfing

surfing the web

swimming

taking classes

talking on the phone

team sports

telling jokes

traveling

treasure hunting

tweeting on Twitter

watching TV

weaving

woodworking

wrapping presents

writing poetry

yo-yo

yoga

Warm-Up

SPACE PREP	PLAYER PREP	PERFORMANCE
0	0	3-5
MINUTES	MINUTES	MINUTES

PLAYERS	DIFFICULTY
2	3

Teach and Practice:

Blocking and Conventions

Characterization

Concentration

Creativity

Ensemble Acting

Group Dynamics

Listening and Silence

Non-vocal Communication

Observation

Physical Control

Plot Structure

Spontaneity

EQUIPMENT
None.

We're Going on a Vacation

Directions

- Divide into pairs where one player is A and the other is B.
- Give each player one card with a hobby on it. This is to be kept secret. (You can use "Real Hobbies" on page 31 or "Unusual and Imaginary Hobbies" on page 33.)
- With the audience facing the playing area, one pair at a time comes up to start a scene entitled "We're Going on a Vacation" in which two old friends plan where to go and what to do.
- As the scene progresses, each secret hobby becomes an important motivation as to where each player wants to go and what he or she wants to do.
- Each person in the pair tries to incorporate his or her guess of the other's hobby into the decision making.

Examples

- A's hobby is swimming, and B's hobby is flirting. As they plan, A is very concerned that they go somewhere on the coast with warmish water. B is mainly concerned that there will be a lot of parties and cause for socializing.
- A's hobby is identifying cars, and B's hobby is scrapbooking. A suggests a road trip, but B will only agree if they go in a van with lots of room and good suspension so she can spread her supplies out. A wants to go to crowded areas so she can see a wide variety of cars, but B would prefer solitude and space with a large table.

Side Coaching

- Listen carefully for all clues you can about your partner's hobby.
- Watch your partner for physical clues.
- Don't hesitate to guess. Your partner's answer will help you get on the right track.

Evaluation/Critique

- Were the pairs able to identify the secret hobby? How?
- What clues were most effective?
- Did the hobbies cause conflict, or were they ultimately complementary?
- How did the pairs reach consensus?

Unusual and Imaginary Hobbies

chanting all day

cleaning/polishing

collecting friends

communing with ghosts/spirits

cross-dressing

dancing nude

eavesdropping

flirting

gazing at crystal balls

identifying types of cars

insulting people

inventing new colors

inventing new languages

learning new languages

making faces

making kites

making masks

marathon sleeping

memorizing entire books

miming

raking leaves

reading tea leaves

rearranging furniture

reporting on what you're wearing

riding cows

roller coaster riding

speed walking

staring at strangers

swinging on a swing

talking to animals

visiting graveyards

visiting thrift shops

watching license plates

wearing wigs

Warm-Up

SPACE PREP	PLAYER PREP	PERFORMANCE
0 MINUTES	0-2 MINUTES	5-7 MINUTES

PLAYERS	DIFFICULTY
3-5	2

Teach and Practice:

Blocking and Conventions

Characterization

Concentration

Creativity

Ensemble Acting

Group Dynamics

Listening and Silence

Non-vocal Communication

Observation

Physical Control

Plot Structure

Spontaneity

EQUIPMENT
None.

Tableaux (Frozen Pictures)

Directions

- Divide into groups of three to five. (Note: Odd-numbered groups make more interesting frozen pictures.)
- Draw the name of one real and one imaginary holiday.
- Each group makes two frozen pictures, one of the real holiday and one of the imaginary one.
- Tableaux are shown to the rest of the group to guess what they might be celebrating.

Examples

- Groundhog Day takes place in the Pennsylvania Park where everyone is gathered around the hutch containing the groundhog.
- New Year's Eve shows a group of friends, arms around each other, singing "Auld Lang Syne." The person in the middle is blowing a noisemaker.
- Girl Scout's Day has someone eating cookies while the others try to grab some out of the box.

Side Coaching

- As a group, think of the things that best define the holiday.
- Go for the obvious!
- Split the obvious hints up so each person is telling part of the story.

Evaluation/Critique

- How did the group portray the holidays in creative ways?
- Were the groupings interesting visually?
- Did the people in the scenes have distinctive characters, or were they all the same types and in the same mood?

Challenges and Refinements

- Redo the holidays with a different interpretation.
- Give each person in the scene a specific personality but one that also fits the scene.

Discussion

- Talk about what makes a holiday unique. Is it a special object? Ritual? Group activity?

Holidays

Traditional Holidays
All Saints Day
April Fool's Day
Arbor Day
Armed Forces Day
Boss' Day
Boxing Day
Carnival/Mardi Gras
Christmas
Cinco de Mayo
Columbus Day
Day of the Dead
Earth Day
Father's Day
Flag Day
Fourth of July
Grandparents Day
Groundhog Day
Guy Fawkes Day
International Children's Day
International Women's Day
Kwanzaa
Labor Day
Martin Luther King's Birthday
May Day
Memorial Day/Decoration Day
Mother's Day
New Year's Day
New Year's Eve
Patriot's Day
Presidents' Day
Secretary's Day
Summer Solstice
Thanksgiving
Valentine's Day
Winter Solstice

Unusual Holidays
American Red Cross Month
Music in Our Schools Month
National Crafts Day
Frozen Food Month
We Love Noodles Day
Good Nutrition Day
Women's History Month
Black History Month
Youth Month
Bubble Gum Week
Newspapers in Our Schools
National Crying Day
Dr. Seuss' Birthday
Dentist Day
Girl Scout Day
Buzzard Day
Good Samaritan Day
Potato Chip Day
Johnny Appleseed Day
National Quilting Day
Swallows Return Day
Big Bird's Birthday
Children's Poetry Day
Sing Out Day
Something on a Stick Day
Poison Prevention Month
Wright Brothers Day
Flag Day

Fantasy Holidays
I Won the Lottery Day
Good Hair Day
New Clothes Day
My Pet's Birthday
I Got Straight As Day
I Lost My First Tooth Day
National Board Game Day
National Dog/Cat Owners Day
National Bad Hair Day
Denim Day
I Love Fruit Day
No Smoking Day
Bad Joke Day
Tea Is Better Than Coffee Day
Umbrella Day
Twins Day
Short People's Day
Redheads Day

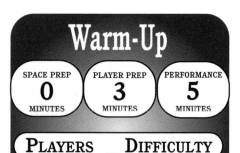

Warm-Up

SPACE PREP	PLAYER PREP	PERFORMANCE
0	**3**	**5**
MINUTES	MINUTES	MINUTES

PLAYERS	DIFFICULTY
3	3

Teach and Practice:

Blocking and Conventions

Characterization

Concentration

Creativity

Ensemble Acting

Group Dynamics

Listening and Silence

Non-vocal Communication

Observation

Physical Control

Plot Structure

Spontaneity

EQUIPMENT

Real purses or backpacks (optional)

3 objects per purse or backpack (optional).

Backpack Game

Directions

- Divide into groups of three.
- Each group receives a backpack or purse. (These may be real or pantomimed.)
- Each backpack or purse has three actual objects or three cards with the names of the objects on them.
- The group has three minutes to prepare a scene using all three objects.

Examples

- Items are a prescription, iPad, and digital camera. One person is a very ill and wants the others to go to the drugstore to fill a prescription for whatever she has. They aren't sure of her malady and check for symptoms on the iPad. Then they take a picture of her on the digital camera to take to the pharmacist to see if the prescription is good for her symptoms.
- Items are a map, phone, and water bottle. The three discover a map rolled up in a water bottle they found on the ground. After studying it closely, they think it must be details of a robbery-to-be. They use their phone to call the police.

Side Coaching

- You don't have to commit to the first idea. You can start by just throwing out ideas, and then choose the best ones.
- Try not to concentrate on one item exclusively. Make sure each item has a good idea.

Evaluation/Critique

- Were all the objects used?
- Were the uses credible? Creative?
- Did the scene make sense?
- Was there any resolution? If not, could it have been resolved? How?

Challenges and Refinements

- Develop the scene into a longer scene with a beginning, middle, and ending.
- Choose one object at random and use this as the introduction to a new scene.

Items in a Purse or Backpack

action figure
airplane ticket
allergy medication
Altoids/breath mints
ankle bracelet
anti-nausea
  medication
aspirin
aviator's goggles
badge
bandages
Barbie doll
binder
biography book
boarding pass
bow tie
box of chocolates
brochure
business cards
buttons
calendar
camera, digital or
  disposable
candy bar
cards, Tarot cards
carnival ride ticket
CD
CD player
Cellophane tape
change purse
check for large sum
checkbook
cheese grater
chess piece
church bulletin
cigarettes
classic book
clothes brush
coffee filter
collapsible cup
comb
commando knife
compass
concert ticket
contact lenses
contract
cotton balls
credit card

cross country ski wax
crossword puzzle
cruise ship ticket
diamond ring
diary, locked
dish towel
doctor's appointment
  card
dog collar
dog leash
"Do Not Disturb" sign
drinking straw
drumsticks
duct tape
DVD
DVD player
earrings
electronic book
  reader, Kindle, Nook
empty CD case
envelopes
extension cord
eye shadow
eyebrow pencil
fan
fantasy book
feather
film camera
first aid kit
flag
flashlight
flask
football game ticket
fork
game book
glasses
glitter
gloves
glue
GPS
greeting cards
guidebook
gun
hair conditioner
hairbrush
hand lotion
handicap placard
handkerchief

hard drive
hat/cap
highlighters
horoscope
horseshoe
hotel key
house key
hunting knife
iPad
index cards
ink bottle
iPod
jewelry
keys, car
kid's book
laser pointer
Legos
letter opener
light bulb
lip balm
lipstick
London A-Z map
lotion
lunch
Mace spray
magazine
map
map of Paris
marbles
markers
mascara
mask
Matryoshka dolls
measuring cup
measuring spoons
memory stick
mini teapot
modeling clay
money clip
mouse
mouse pad
movie ticket
MP3 player
mystery book
nail clippers
nail file
nail polish
napkin rings

necklace
newspaper
newspaper clipping
note cards
notepad
opera program
opera ticket
overdue bill
painkillers
pantyhose
paper clips
paper napkin
party horn
passport
passport in someone
  else's name
pen
pencil
pepper grinder
pepper shaker
pepper spray
perfume
phone
Play-Doh
playing cards
popsicle stick
postcards
Post-its
prescription medication
puppet
rabbit's foot
rain jacket
razor
receipts
religious icon
remote control for
  garage door
rock concert ticket
rocks
romance book
rubber stamp
safe deposit box key
salt shaker
scarf
science fiction book
seed packet

self-improvement
  book
sewing kit
shampoo
shawl
shells
shower cap
slippers
snake bite kit
snorkel
soap
socks
speeding ticket
stamps
stapler
staples
string
subway ticket
sunglasses
sunscreen
suntan lotion
swim cap
swim goggles
swimsuit
table knife
teabags
theatre program
theatre ticket
thermometer
thermos
tissue
true crime book
Tupperware
TV remote control
umbrella
underwear
video camera
wallet
water bottle
watercolors
whip
whistle
will
wine bottle
wrapped present

Warm-Up

SPACE PREP	PLAYER PREP	PERFORMANCE
0	**0**	**3-5**
MINUTES	MINUTES	MINUTES

PLAYERS	DIFFICULTY
2	**2**

Teach and Practice:

Blocking and Conventions

Characterization

Concentration

Creativity

Ensemble Acting

Group Dynamics

Listening and Silence

Non-vocal Communication

Observation

Physical Control

Plot Structure

Spontaneity

EQUIPMENT
None.

Let the Games Begin

Directions

- Divide the group into pairs.
- Each pair decides who will be the commentator and who will be the Olympian.
- Each pair receives the name of a real Olympic event.
- Starting with a freeze, the commentator describes what the Olympian is doing as the Olympian accomplishes the task as simultaneously as possible for a one-minute scene.
- Trade jobs and repeat.

Example

The fencing freeze starts with the *en garde* position and then goes into a series of fencing movements (which may or may not be accurate) as they are described by the commentator.

Side Coaching

- Olympian — Follow the description!
- Commentator — Clearly define and describe the movements!

Evaluation/Critique

- Were the movements clearly recognizable?
- Did the comments match the movement or suggest new ones?
- Did the two follow each other so that eventually you didn't know who was leading?

Challenges and Refinements

- (Easier) The Olympian originates the movement and the commentator describes them for a radio audience.
- (More Difficult) The Olympian does the movements as described by the commentator in real time, then instantly replays in slow motion. (This may reveal unseen actions.)
- (More Difficult Yet) Same idea, but introduce more than one player for team sports.
- (Zanier) The game is played with an imaginary/non-Olympic sport described by the commentator and played by the Olympian.
- (Zaniest) The game is played with an imaginary/non-Olympic sport with slow motion replays narrated by the commentator.

Olympic Sports

Real Olympic Sports (Current, Historic, Exhibition)

alpine skiing

archery

badminton

baseball

beach volleyball

biathlon

billiards

bobsled

boxing

canoe/kayak slalom

canoe/kayak sprint

chess

climbing

cricket

croquet

cross country skiing

curling

cycling, track

cycling, BMX

cycling, mountain bike

cycling, road

dance

decathlon

discus throw

diving

equestrian, dressage

equestrian, eventing

equestrian, jumping

fencing

field hockey

figure skating

football

freestyle skiing

golf

gymnastics

hammer throw

handball

heptathlon

high jump

hockey

hurdles

ice hockey

javelin throw

judo

jumping

karate

kayaking

lacrosse

long jump

luge

netball

pentathlon

pole vault

polo

racquetball

relay

rhythmic gymnastics

rowing

rugby

running, long distance

running, marathon

running, short sprint

sailing

shooting

shotput

skating

skiing, snow

skiing, water

ski jumping

snowboarding

softball

speed skating

squash

steeplechase

swimming

table tennis

tennis

triathlon

volleyball

water polo

weight lifting

wrestling, freestyle

wrestling, sumo

Imaginary and Non-Olympic Sports

barn mucking

body contortions

bungee jumping

breath holding

butterfly catching

caber throwing

cat washing

clothes folding

clumsy dancing

cotton candy eating

dog chasing

dog washing

eating quickly

egg teaspoon racing

egg tossing

fire juggling

fire starting with two sticks

free diving

funny face making

garbage collecting

hair styling

hot dog eating

knot tying

knot untying

lawn mowing

lion taming

magic card tricks

nail polishing

petunia planting

poetry reciting

poker cheating

roller coaster riding

rolling down hills

racing

sack racing

sidewalk chalk art

silent screaming

speed bathing

speed dressing

speed reading

speed typing

stick horse polo

teeth cleaning

three-legged racing

tongue twisters

tug-of-war

underwater basket weaving

underwater kissing

watermelon eating

wheelbarrow racing

Warm-Up

SPACE PREP	PLAYER PREP	PERFORMANCE
0	0	3-5
MINUTES	MINUTES	MINUTES

PLAYERS	DIFFICULTY
1	3

Teach and Practice:

Blocking and Conventions

Characterization

Concentration

Creativity

Ensemble Acting

Group Dynamics

Listening and Silence

Non-vocal Communication

Observation

Physical Control

Plot Structure

Spontaneity

EQUIPMENT

None.

I've Got the Message

Directions

- One at a time, players draw a kind of phone call out of a hat.
- Player must immediately pick up the phone and react to the message without explicitly stating what is being said.
- The audience guesses what the call was.

Examples

- The call is about a friend in the ICU. The player answers the call cheerfully, but then he doesn't seem to be able to process what is being said. He gets more and more upset before he thinks to ask for details.
- The call is from a breather. The player answers cheerfully, but first thinks he cannot hear properly. He shields the phone, moves to a different part of the room, and asks the person to repeat. Finally, he gets angry and then scared.

Side Coaching

- Respond with your body to the message.
- Let your voice reflect your emotions as you react.
- Ask questions and make statements that let us know what the call is regarding.

Evaluation/Critique

- How much was communicated non-vocally? Vocally?
- Did the player use pause to good effect?
- How did the player manage to show what was being said without telling?

Challenges and Refinements

- The player may react totally non-vocally or by using only sounds.
- The scene can be developed to add what happens after the call.
- Other actors may join in.

Phone Calls

aggressive phone solicitation

bank robber being caught in your apartment
   complex

being fired

best friend moving to another state
   or country

bid on a house not being accepted

book you ordered has arrived at the
   bookstore

"breather"

call from a long-lost friend

call from nursery school to say your child
   is sick

call from someone who does not speak your
   language, but is obviously in trouble

cancellation of an important flight
   to a conference

decision to tear your house down for
   the new airport

fifty pounds of frozen fish that you didn't
   order is ready to be picked up

fight your child was in at school

friend in intensive care

getting accepted into the college you wanted

getting the job you wanted

getting the lead in a musical

gossip about a close friend who has done
   something strange

mail being delivered to someone in another
   part of town

missed ear/nose/throat doctor's appointment

missed endoscopy doctor's appointment

prank phone call that turns ugly

significant other breaking up with you

someone finding your lost dog

threatening phone call

winning a big scholarship

winning the lottery

your ride will be half an hour late picking
   you up for school

your stolen car has been recovered

Warm-Up

SPACE PREP	PLAYER PREP	PERFORMANCE
0	0	1
MINUTES	MINUTES	MINUTES

PLAYERS	DIFFICULTY
2	2

Teach and Practice:

Blocking and Conventions

Characterization

Concentration

Creativity

Ensemble Acting

Group Dynamics

Listening and Silence

Non-vocal Communication

Observation

Physical Control

Plot Structure

Spontaneity

EQUIPMENT
None.

Preposition Game

Directions

- The director divides the group into pairs.
- The director gives each pair three prepositions.
- Each pair is to use all three of their prepositions in a one-minute, non-rehearsed scene.

Examples

- Prepositions are "near," "onto," and "above." They choose a scene at a zoo where two mischievous children try to get near a gorilla's cage and end up climbing on the overhead bars.
- Prepositions are "outside," "ahead of," and "beside." They act out a scene about two siblings on the way to school. First, they push their way outside and then start to race each other down the sidewalk. When one gets way behind, the other slows to walk beside her.

Side Coaching

- Most prepositions show a physical relationship to something — use that.
- Go with your first instinct with your preposition. You can refine later.
- Watch your partner for visual cues to play off.

Evaluation/Critique

- Did the prepositions suggest types of movement?
- Did the prepositions suggest types of activities?
- Were the scenes coherent? Did they make sense?
- Were the prepositions used clearly? Did the use of prepositions enhance the scene? How?

Challenges and Refinements

- Build a longer scene using the prepositions and a character element. (See "Relationships" on page 85, "Stereotypes" on page 90, "Chinese Astrological Types" on page 64, or "Western Astrological Types" on page 100 for character ideas.)
- Use one or two props in the scene to demonstrate the preposition. (See "Items in a Purse or Backpack" on page 37, "Utensils" on page 53, or "Exhibitions and Collections" on page 24 for prop ideas.)

Prepositions

aboard
about
above
according to
across
after
against
ahead of
along
along with
alongside
amid
among
apart from
around
as
aside
aside from
astride
at
atop
away
away from
before
behind
below
beneath
beside
besides
between
beyond
by
by means of

circa
close to
concerning
considering
contrary to
counting
depending on
despite
down
due to
during
except
except for
excluding
far from
following
for
forward
from
further
given
in
in addition to
in back of
in between
in case of
in favor of
in front of
in place
in place of
in spite of
in view of
including

inside
inside of
instead of
into
less
like
minus
near
next
next to
of
off
on
on account of
on behalf of
on board
on to
on top of
onto
opposite
other than
out
out of
outside
over
past
per
plus
prior to
regarding
regardless of
respecting
round

save
save for
saving
since
than
thanks to
through
throughout
to
together with
touching
toward
under
underneath
unlike
until
up
up against
up to
up until
upon
versus
with
within
without
worth

Warm-Up

SPACE PREP	PLAYER PREP	PERFORMANCE
0 MINUTES	**0** MINUTES	**5** MINUTES

PLAYERS	DIFFICULTY
4	2

Teach and Practice:

Blocking and Conventions

Characterization

Concentration

Creativity

Ensemble Acting

Group Dynamics

Listening and Silence

Non-vocal Communication

Observation

Physical Control

Plot Structure

Spontaneity

EQUIPMENT

None.

And the Winner Is ...

Directions

- Divide into groups of four.
- One member is chosen as a talk-show host. The host draws one card with an award for each guest, and another card saying "best" or "worst." Only the host knows each guest's award. (Optional: The host may share with the audience, not the guests.)
- The three guests have received awards which they are on the talk show to discuss. As each guest comes on, the host talks to him about the award, why he won it and what it might mean to him. During this process the host gives enough hints through the discussion that the guest may answer logically and finally guess what his award is.
- The other guests may join in, and questions may be taken from the group watching.
- Award recipients may be asked to do demonstrations of the activity that garnered them the awards.

Example

The award is for the best groupie. Questions include: How did the guest become involved with music? How long has the guest been doing this? Isn't it exhausting? Just what does someone on the edge of a music group do? Does the guest do this for all musical groups or only one?

Side Coaching

- Host — Ask leading questions without telling the guest directly.
- Host — Focus on the type of award.
- Guest — Don't be timid. Take a chance with your answers.

Evaluation/Critique

- Was the host able to ask interesting questions that called for in-depth answers?
- Were the recipients able to answer in a seemingly logical manner and to explain fully?
- Were the explanations creative?
- Did the host and guest have personalities unique to their roles?

Prizes for Best and Worst

advertisement

athlete

bachelor(ette) party

behaved student

book

celebrity

child

Christmas present

college major

color

conversationalist

cook

doctor

dresser

driver

event

film

film kiss

friend

gossip

groomed

groupie

horror film

looking

magazine

mascot

news headline

news story of the year

newscaster

opera

perfume

pet

pet owner

prank phone call

question

quiz show

reality TV celebrity

reality TV show

restaurant

sentence

shrink

sibling

smelling

snob

song

sport

spouse

student of _____ (subject)

style

surprise party

toy

TV show

PLAYERS	DIFFICULTY
3-5	3

Teach and Practice:

Blocking and Conventions

Characterization

Concentration

Creativity

Ensemble Acting

Group Dynamics

Listening and Silence

Non-vocal Communication

Observation

Physical Control

Plot Structure

Spontaneity

EQUIPMENT
None.

Musical Comedy

Directions

- Divide into groups of three to five.
- Each group receives a song title and a song style.
- Groups get five minutes to plan a scene in which the group breaks into that song sung in that style.

Examples

- Song: "My Rubber Ball." Style: patriotic. The group develops a scene in which a group of people from some unknown country are planning to rewrite their national anthem for the Olympics.
- Song: "Never." Style: hard rock. The group devises a scene in which a boy is trying to flirt with a girl who is totally not interested in him. She and her girl friend(s) sing the song to get him to leave her alone.

Side Coaching

- Voices aren't the concern in this scene. Just sing it!
- Don't forget the kind of song it is. Work in that style.
- Remember the title. Make sure your scene fits.

Evaluation/Critique

- Did the songs fit the scenes?
- Did the styles fit the titles?
- Did the scenes make sense?

Challenges and Refinements

- Develop a short musical in the same musical style or using two or three different styles.

Song Titles and Styles

Titles

A Change Is
  Gonna Come
All about You
Alone Together
Alone with You
Amazed
Backbite
Becky's Blues
Being Human
Believe in Me
Betrayed
Big Bully Blues
Birds and Bees
Birdsong
Blowin' in the Wind
Blue
Blue Suede Shoes
Brainstormin'
Break It Off
Break It Up
Bridesmaid's Blues
Clueless
Confusion
Coyote Calls
Cry Alone
Don't Go from Me
Dreams of You
Dry Rot
Dust
Dust in the Wind
Every Single Day
Feedback
Feelin' Good
Forever Blue
Forget about Me
Forget Me
Good Vibrations
Heartburn
Hey Jude
Hidden from You

Hound Dog
I Want to Hold
  Your Hand
I Wonder
Imagine
In a Deep Dark
  Forest
In the Loop de Loop
Is This It?
It's Natural
Jail Break
Jester's Lament
Johnny B. Goode
Later Love
Later Next Week
Laundromat Lament
Leave!
Left
Legos
Let It Be
Let Me Go
Let Me Know
Let's Do It!
Let's Try Again
Light as a Feather
Like a Rolling Stone
London Calling
Lonely Me
Lonely One
Losing It
Lost Forever
Lost in You
Lost Marbles
Love in the Air
Lover's Lament
Man of My Dreams
Manhandled
Maybelline
Mind Blowing
Mind Control
Morning Zombie

My Generation
My Rubber Ball
Never
Never Again
Nevermore
No Regrets
Not Again
Only Me
Out of Sight
Over and Over
Owl's Cry
Playin' with
  My Mind
Please Return
Pulling Through
Purple Haze
Random Acts
Regrets
Repetition
Respect
Return to Me
Return to Sender
Road Rage
Roller Coaster
Satisfaction
Schoolhouse Blues
Sever the Ties
Shame on You
Sledgehammer Blues
Sleepless Nights
Smells Like Teen
  Spirit
So Alone
Song at Sunrise
Song for Charlotte
Song for Sara
Song of Sorrow
Sunrise, Sunset
Surprise
Surprise Party
Surrender

Teardrop Serenade
Tell the Truth
The Loner
The Only One
Try It on for Size
Tsunami Fever
Tunnel Vision
Undeserved
Unexpected Love
Unforgettable
Valentine's Day
  Blues
Valhalla Dreams
Wake Up Call
Water over the
  Bridge
We Are the
  Champions
What Goes Around
What'd I Say
What's Going On
Where Are You?
Why?
Why Not?
Wicked Lies
Wild Ones
Winner's Waltz
Wrap It Up
Written in Stone
Yesterday
You
You Rock Me

Styles

art song
baroque
bluegrass
blues
Celtic
Celtic rock
classical
country western
cowboy
disco
dubstep
easy listening
elevator
folk
folk rock
gospel
Gregorian chant
hard rock
Hawaiian
hip-hop
hoedown
hymn
inspirational
Irish drinking
jazz
Latin
lounge
love song
marching song
Mariachi
opera
patriotic
polka
pop
progressive rock
punk
rap
rhythm and blues
rock and roll
rockabilly
salsa
soul
spiritual
swing
techno

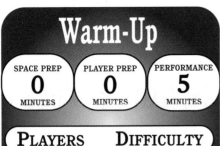

Warm-Up

SPACE PREP	PLAYER PREP	PERFORMANCE
0	0	5
MINUTES	MINUTES	MINUTES

PLAYERS	DIFFICULTY
2	2

Teach and Practice:

Blocking and Conventions

Characterization

Concentration

Creativity

Ensemble Acting

Group Dynamics

Listening and Silence

Non-vocal Communication

Observation

Physical Control

Plot Structure

Spontaneity

EQUIPMENT
None.

My Pet Boa

Directions
- Divide the group into As and Bs. Half the As and half the Bs line up on two sides of the playing area. The rest of the group watches.
- Each player is given the name of a strange pet. (Note: This may be an animal or an object.)
- The players approach each other from opposite sides with their "pets," handling them appropriately.
- They need to discover what the other player's pet is and to interact with it and their own pet.
- Play ends when both pets are known and interact.
- After the entire first group performs, the second group of As and Bs repeats the process.

Examples
- Player A has a pet boa, and Player B has a pet cow. Player A tries desperately to keep the boa from attacking the cow while apologizing for its behavior. Player B is having difficulty with the cow because she needs to be milked.
- Player A has a stuffed bunny, and Player B has a kangaroo. Player A is cuddling the bunny as Player B is trying to keep the kangaroo from hopping away. Eventually, the bunny is put in the kangaroo's pocket, and all is well.

Side Coaching
- Don't forget to interact with your own pet, the other player, and the other player's pet.
- Go ahead and interact with the other player's pet. Your partner will help you with it.

Evaluation/Critique
- How were the clues revealed?
- Which clues worked and which ones didn't? Why?
- How were clues shown but not told?
- How quickly did the pair find ways to have their pets interact? Or did they not?
- Was the scene ended/resolved? How?

Challenges and Refinements
- Develop a serious conflict in the scene and resolve it.
- Use the conflict as a crisis point, and end the scene there.
- Use the conflict as a way to unite/destroy As and Bs relationship.

Animal Pets

anaconda
banana slug
bear
boa constrictor
chameleon
chicken
cobra
cow
dolphin
eagle
falcon
fish
flea
kangaroo
Komodo dragon
lion
manatee
mink
mosquito
pig
pit bull
poodle
raccoon
rat iguana
raven
rhinoceros
salamander
scorpion
skunk
snail
spider
squirrel
whale
wolf
wombat

Non-Animal Pets

action figure
balloon toy
Barbie doll
blocks
boom box
cactus
clown
cookie cutter
CPR doll
dishcloth
flower
gumball machine
handkerchief
hobby horse
iPad
lipstick
mask
microphone
mini car
monkey's paw
paperweight
perfume
piece of fur
plant
pot roast
puppet/marionette
rabbit's foot
rock
rocking horse
rubber band
shamrock
shell
skull
straw
stuffed bunny
teddy bear
water bottle
wooden figure

Warm-Up

SPACE PREP	PLAYER PREP	PERFORMANCE
0	0	5
MINUTES	MINUTES	MINUTES

PLAYERS	DIFFICULTY
Full Group	1

Teach and Practice:

Blocking and Conventions

Characterization

Concentration

Creativity

Ensemble Acting

Group Dynamics

Listening and Silence

Non-vocal Communication

Observation

Physical Control

Plot Structure

Spontaneity

EQUIPMENT
Ball.

A Touch Of ...

Directions

- The group stands in a circle.
- The director passes a ball to the person on his or her right, calling out a texture. The person receives the ball as if it is that texture.
- The person then passes the ball to the next person who receives it as that same texture.
- The director changes the texture every five or six players or as seems workable.
- The play continues as the director calls out different textures, and the passing continues.

Side Coaching

- Use your five senses!
- Don't just rely on touch!
- Make your movements and facial expressions broad!
- Add sounds as you interact with the ball!
- Examine the variety of the texture!

Evaluation/Critique

- Was there a variety of ways to experience each texture?
- Did the texture bring up any emotions?
- Did each person do something different with the ball?

abrasive

barbed

bendable

blistered

bulging

bulky

bumpy

burning

carved

chunky

coarse

cold

corduroy

corrugated

damp

dented

dirty

dripping

dusty

etched

filmy

fluffy

furry

fuzzy

gelatinous

glossy

gooey

gritty

icy

itchy

jagged

moist

mushy

ornamented

padded

pitted

pleated

pointy

prickly

pulpy

razor sharp

ribbed

rigid

rough

scalding

silky

slick

slippery

smooth

soft

soggy

stiff

tacky

thick

thin

uneven

velvety

wet

wide

wooly

woven

Warm-Up

SPACE PREP	PLAYER PREP	PERFORMANCE
0	0	5
MINUTES	MINUTES	MINUTES

PLAYERS	DIFFICULTY
Full Group	1

Teach and Practice:

Blocking and Conventions

Characterization

Concentration

Creativity

Ensemble Acting

Group Dynamics

Listening and Silence

Non-vocal Communication

Observation

Physical Control

Plot Structure

Spontaneity

EQUIPMENT
Assortment of utensils.

Useful Utensils

Directions
- The group stands in a circle.
- Director demonstrates common usage of utensils provided.
- Director challenges players to think of other possible uses for the utensil.
- Director passes utensil to the right. The player has to use it as something other than what it really is.
- Play continues around the circle until everyone has had an opportunity to invent a use for the utensil.

Examples
- A basting brush might be used as a shaving brush or an eyelash curler.
- A cauldron could be used as a bathtub or cereal bowl.

Side Coaching
- Go with your first instinct.
- If nothing "normal" comes, try something far out.

Evaluation/Critique
- Did the shape of the object suggest the uses?
- Were the less obvious uses plausible?

basting brush
basting syringe
blender
bowl
bread board
bread knife
bread machine
butcher block
cake pan
cake server
can opener
candy thermometer
casserole
cauldron
cheese cutter
chef's knife
chopsticks
coffee maker
colander
cookie cutter
cookie sheet
Crock-Pot
cutting board
double boiler
egg beater
egg poacher
egg separator
fat separator
fork
frying pan
garlic press
grater
griddle
grill
herb chopper
kitchen scale
kitchen scissors
ladle
lemon zester
measuring cup

measuring spoons
microwave oven
mixing bowl
mortar and pestle
muffin cups
muffin tin
nutcracker
oven mitts
pancake forms
pastry bag
pastry brush
pepper mill
pie pan
pizza cutter
potholder
potato masher
potato peeler
potato ricer
pressure cooker
rolling pin
salad tongs
salt shaker
saucepan
scoop
sifter
skillet
slotted spoon
spatula
spoon
strainer
tea kettle
teapot
timer
toaster
toaster oven
tongs
waffle iron
whisk
wooden spoon

Warm-Up

SPACE PREP	PLAYER PREP	PERFORMANCE
0 MINUTES	**0** MINUTES	**3-5** MINUTES

PLAYERS	DIFFICULTY
2	2

Teach and Practice:

Blocking and Conventions

Characterization

Concentration

Creativity

Ensemble Acting

Group Dynamics

Listening and Silence

Non-vocal Communication

Observation

Physical Control

Plot Structure

Spontaneity

EQUIPMENT
None.

Why Can't I?

Directions

• Divide into pairs.
• Give each pair four "whines" on cards.
• The object is for each pair to incorporate all of the whines into a scene of their choosing or into a generic scene chosen by the director.

Examples

• Whines are "That's what you think," "You're so out of it," "No way," and "I can't hear you." The players decide on a mother/daughter scene in which the daughter wants to stay out late and the mother will not allow it.
• Whines are "Leave me alone," "Nobody likes me," "Get away," and "Why can't I?" The pair decides on a scene where one is on a ledge thinking of jumping and the other is trying to understand and help.

Side Coaching

• Make sure your whines are motivated and logical, not just out of the blue.

Evaluation/Critique

• Were the whines logically incorporated into the scene?
• Did the whines move the scene forward?
• Did each player have a distinct character?
• Did the scene have a beginning, middle, and ending?

Challenges and Refinements

• Using the same whines, play a new scene that uses no other words but those given on the cards.

Because I said so.

Don't you dare.

Don't you dare talk to me like that.

Everyone else does.

Get away.

Get out.

Get out of here.

Get out of my room.

Go away.

Go to your room.

I can't believe you did that.

I can't hear you.

I don't believe you just said that.

I don't want to hear another word.

I won't!

Leave me alone.

Never again.

No way.

Nobody likes me.

Not a chance.

Not again.

Oh, you think so, do you?

One more word out of you …

That's it.

That's the stupidest thing I've ever heard.

That's what you think.

There you go again.

Try me.

Why can't I?

Why can't you just grow up?

You are so out of it.

You can't make me!

You don't understand.

You don't understand me.

You just don't get it, do you?

You make me sick.

You never listen to me.

Characterization

There are many ways of developing a character. Perhaps the two most common are from the outside in or from the inside out. Examples of the former include non-vocal cues, such as ways of walking, dressing, and gesturing to begin to build the character's persona. Examples of the latter include presenting types and temperament. A third way, less common and even more challenging, is to build a character relationally based on how that character relates to others and to situations.

No matter how one chooses to build a character, the whole person must be kept in mind. This includes the physical, mental, and emotional life of the character, or the internal and external worlds of the person. This may touch on the questions of nature or nurture. It can get very complicated!

For the purposes of this book, characterization will be presented in its simplest forms. These games and lists do not claim to go into deep psychological territory. That is for another type of book. Just touching the basics, we hope that you can see glimmers of how complex character building may be and what might go into shaping a full-blown character on the stage.

Characterization at a Glance

Game	Page	Space Prep	Player Prep	Performance	Group Size	Blocking and Conventions	Characterization	Concentration	Creativity	Ensemble Acting	Group Dynamics	Listening and Silence	Non-Vocal Communication	Observation	Physical Control	Plot Structure	Spontaneity	Equipment
Faculty Meeting	59	0	1	3-5	4		●	●	●	●	●		●				●	
What's Wrong with Me?	61	0	1	2-3	2		●	●	●			●	●	●	●		●	●
I'm an Ox!	63	0	1	3-4	2		●	●	●				●				●	
Clothes Make the Person	65	0	2	2-3	2		●		●				●	●			●	●
Color Me Pink	68	0	2	2-3	2		●		●				●	●			●	
Friends Forever	70	0	0	2-3	2		●		●				●	●			●	
High Five!	72	0	1	1-2	2		●	●	●				●	●	●		●	
My Tiara	74	0	0	2-3	2		●		●				●				●	opt.
Please and Thank You	76	0	1	2-3	4		●		●	●			●	●			●	
In the Mood	78	0	0	3-5	2		●		●				●				●	
Phobia Game	80	0	2	2-3	2		●	●	●				●	●			●	
Relationship Dyads	84	0	1	2-3	2		●		●				●				●	
Skillful	86	0	2	3-5	2+		●	●	●				●			●	●	
Valley Girls vs. Snobs	89	0	0	3-4	2+		●		●	●			●			●	●	
It's My Name!	91	0	0	3-4	2		●		●				●			●	●	
Job Interview	93	0	0	3-5	2		●	●	●				●				●	
Devil Made Me Do It	95	0	0	2-3	2		●		●				●			●	●	
Virtuous Family	97	0	1	2-3	4		●		●	●	●		●	●		●	●	
Trapped with a Libra	99	0	1	2-3	2		●		●				●	●		●	●	

Faculty Meeting

Characterization

SPACE PREP	PLAYER PREP	PERFORMANCE
0	1	3-5
MINUTES	MINUTES	MINUTES

PLAYERS

4

Directions

- Divide into groups of four.
- The setting is a meeting room at a university or college. One player is the moderator, and each of the other players is given an academic discipline. Their roles are as professors of those disciplines, and they may play stereotypes.
- The scene is a meeting to discuss cutbacks. One of the programs needs to be dropped. The professors must argue for keeping their own programs.
- They have one minute to prepare and three minutes to perform the scene.

Examples

- Disciplines: French, education, and women's studies. The French professor is very elitist, the education professor is earnest, and the women's studies professor is angry.
- Disciplines: law, English literature, and journalism. The law professor is career-oriented, the English professor is otherworldly, and the journalism professor joins forces with the law professor on the grounds of real-world skills.

Side Coaching

- This is your job. Fight for it!
- This is war. Cut the other departments down while you build yours up!

Evaluation/Critique

- What physical/vocal qualities helped define the characters?
- Did the qualities go beyond obvious stereotypes? In what way?

Challenges and Refinements

- Put the same characters in different situations: a job interview, a first date, speaking to a class.
- Interview these characters on a talk show as to why they chose their occupations.
- Have a professor try to convince a prospective student to major in his or her academic area.

Teach and Practice:

Blocking and Conventions

Characterization

Concentration

Creativity

Ensemble Acting

Group Dynamics

Listening and Silence

Non-vocal Communication

Observation

Physical Control

Plot Structure

Spontaneity

EQUIPMENT
None.

Academic Disciplines

African American studies

agriculture

American history

ancient history

anthropology

applied mathematics

applied physics

archaeology

architecture

area studies

astrophysics

behavioral psychology

biology

botany

business

chemistry

Chinese

climate studies

clinical psychology

computer science

conflict studies

criminal justice

cultural/ethnic studies

diversity

earth science

economics

education

engineering

English literature

environment

family and consumer studies

French

gender studies

geography

geology

German

graphic design

health sciences

history

Italian

journalism

Latin studies

law

LGBT studies

library science/museum curating

life science

linguistics

logic

mathematics

media studies

meteorology

military sciences

music, band

music, orchestra

music, vocal

oceanography

painting

performing arts

philosophy

photography

physical education

physics

political science

politics

psychology

public administration

religion

Russian

social work

sociology

soil and crop sciences

space/aeronautics

Spanish

statistics

theatre

theoretical physics

transportation

visual arts

women's studies

world literature

zoology

What's Wrong with Me?

Directions

- Two at a time, players sit on the bench in a park and draw an annoying medical condition. They share their conditions silently and prepare for one minute.
- The players create their own characters and reason for being in the park.
- The two players perform a scene in which they try to hide their conditions at first, but then the conditions gradually escalate until their conditions take over the players' personalities.

Examples

- A little kid has bad breath, and an old lady has a bad knee. The child sits down close to the old lady who moves away. The child keeps getting closer and it becomes more and more difficult for the old lady to avoid the bad breath. She is having difficulty getting up and leaving, though, because of her knee.
- A woman eating her lunch on the bench has acid reflux, and a person reading next to her has bad dandruff. The woman is having difficulty swallowing. She happens to look over at the person with dandruff, who is patting it off her shoulders, and it makes the woman gag and aggravates the acid reflux.

Side Coaching

- Play your own condition, but be aware of the other person's!
- Gradually give in to your condition. Let it eventually consume you!

Evaluation/Critique

- Was the medical condition a part of the character's personality? How? What did it motivate the character to do or not do?
- Did the medical condition determine the action? Cause conflict?

Teach and Practice:

Blocking and Conventions

Characterization

Concentration

Creativity

Ensemble Acting

Group Dynamics

Listening and Silence

Non-vocal Communication

Observation

Physical Control

Plot Structure

Spontaneity

EQUIPMENT
Bench.

Use this game with kindness and discuss beforehand that many people do have these problems, and for some, they can be quite serious.

Annoying Medical Conditions

acid reflux

acne

allergies

altitude sickness

arthritis

asthma

back pain

bad breath

bad knee

baldness

burns

canker sores

dandruff

ear infection

flatulence

flu

fracture

gum disease

headache

hearing loss

heat stroke

heel pain

hives

ingrown toenail

joint pain

limp

mononucleosis

muscle cramps

muscle pain

nail biting

narcolepsy

neck pain

panic attack

pink eye

poor uncorrected eyesight

post-nasal drip

restless leg syndrome

skin rash

sleep apnea

snoring

sore throat

stiff neck

sun sensitivity

tennis elbow

tooth decay

I'm an Ox!

Directions

- Divide into pairs.
- Each player draws a Chinese zodiac animal with characteristics. (Optional: Read the story of how the "Animals of the Chinese Zodiac" raced on page 157.)
- With one minute of prep time, the pair plays a generic scene in which they meet and interact. (See page 18 for "Generic Scenes" or refer to *Improv Ideas,* page 71.)
- The scene should stress a beginning, a middle, and an ending.

Examples

- The Ox meets the Monkey taking a test. The Ox sits down and diligently puts his school supplies out on the desk in front of him. He clears his mind and sits waiting for the test to begin. He looks at his watch. The Monkey sits next to him, cracking jokes that annoy the Ox. When the test starts, the Monkey tries to look at the Ox's test, only to be rebuffed. Undeterred, he applies himself and finishes long before the Ox.
- The Tiger meets the Dog on a first date. The Tiger arrives at the Dog's front door in a sports car, slicking back his hair. The door opens, and the Tiger approaches the Dog, saying, "Wow! Better than I thought." The Dog is taken aback and uncomfortable, but tries to be nice to the Tiger as they get into his car. She asks many questions about the car, his driving, and his reasons for driving such a car, but goes with him anyway.

Side Coaching

- Use both mental and physical attributes of your animal.
- Keep asking, "How would I act as this animal?"
- Explore subtle as well as obvious attributes.

Evaluation/Critique

- Were the two types clearly distinguished?
- Did their individual characteristics lead to conflict?
- Was this conflict resolved? Did their personality traits show different ways of resolving the conflict?

Challenges and Refinements

- Give the animal types some of the physical characteristics of the animal in human form. (The Rat is fidgety and quiet; the Ox is large, slow, and steady, etc.)

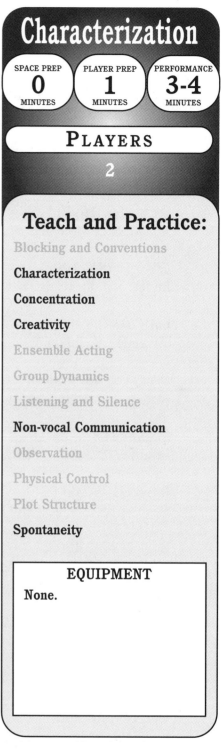

Characterization

SPACE PREP	PLAYER PREP	PERFORMANCE
0	1	3-4
MINUTES	MINUTES	MINUTES

PLAYERS
2

Teach and Practice:

Blocking and Conventions

Characterization

Concentration

Creativity

Ensemble Acting

Group Dynamics

Listening and Silence

Non-vocal Communication

Observation

Physical Control

Plot Structure

Spontaneity

EQUIPMENT
None.

Chinese Astrological Types

Rat (1984, 1996)
Social, intellectual, skilled, charismatic, acquisitive, talkative, pleasant, good provider.

Ox (1985, 1997)
Stable, innovative, eloquent, stubborn, hard worker, serious, diligent.

Tiger (1986, 1998)
Impetuous, lucky, magnetic personality, passionate, honest.

Cat (1987, 1999)
Virtuous, tactful, ambitious, refined, elegant, traditional.

Dragon (1987, 2000)
Strong, successful, healthy, enthusiastic, sentimental, authoritative.

Snake (1989, 2001)
Intuitive, attractive, discreet, thoughtful, successful.

Horse (1990, 2002)
Popular, stylish, accomplished, independent, pragmatic.

Goat (1991, 2003)
Inventive, sensitive, needs security, impractical, slow starter, well-mannered.

Monkey (1992, 2004)
Cunning, enthusiastic, leader, charming, jokester, problem-solver.

Rooster (1993, 2005)
Enthusiastic, conservative, humorous, stylish, helpful, security conscious.

Dog (1994, 2006)
Constant, respectable, dutiful, moral, suspicious, intractable.

Pig (1995, 2007)
Sincere, cultured, honest, strong, loving, luxury seeking, craves knowledge, hot-tempered.

Clothes Make the Person

Characterization

SPACE PREP	PLAYER PREP	PERFORMANCE
0	**2**	**2-3**
MINUTES	MINUTES	MINUTES

PLAYERS

2

Directions

- Put an assortment of clothing in the middle of the playing space, and have each player take one at random. Players put on the clothing if possible.
- Divide the group in pairs.
- Players enter the playing area in pairs and meet. If the garment can't be worn, the player places it near the playing area, and it will be assumed that it is worn.
- They play a one-minute scene incorporating their clothing into their situation and character.

Examples

- One player is in hot pants, and the other is in army boots. The girl in hot pants is a gum-chewing preteen trying to impress. The teenage boy in army boots is very attentive and interested in her.
- One player is in a gym suit, and the other is in pajamas. The person in the gym suit is jogging in place early in the morning. The one in pajamas is out looking for her dog that escaped from the yard when she went to get the paper. The jogger agrees to help find the dog.

Side Coaching

- Feel yourself inside your garment. How much does it weigh? What is the texture?
- Let how your garment fits determine how you move.
- Let the kind of clothing drive how you act. Are you comfortable?

Evaluation/Critique

- Did the item of clothing help suggest a character? How?
- Did the item of clothing help suggest plot? How?
- Did the item of clothing contribute to a conflict?
- Did the players use their items of clothing to move and/or act differently?

Challenges and Refinements

- Players simply draw a card naming a garment or accessory, share it with their partner and the audience, and play the scene as directed.
- An interesting exercise might be to ask the players to bring the most unique piece of clothing that they have to the next session.

Teach and Practice:

Blocking and Conventions

Characterization

Concentration

Creativity

Ensemble Acting

Group Dynamics

Listening and Silence

Non-vocal Communication

Observation

Physical Control

Plot Structure

Spontaneity

EQUIPMENT

Assortment of clothing.

Clothing

alpine hat
ankle boots
Arab headdress
army boots
army helmet
Asian sun hat
astrakhan hat
athletic shoes
aviator cap
baby bonnet
balaclava
ball gown
ballet slippers
baseball cap
bathing suit
belt
beret
Bermuda shorts
bike helmet
bikini
bishop's mitre
boat shoes
bonnet
bowtie
bowling shoes
bridal gown
bridal veil
burka
caftan
camisole
camouflage army hat
cap
cardigan
cargo pants
cavalier

chain mesh hood
character shoes
Charleston flapper headband
chauffeur's cap
chef's toque
clam diggers
cloche
clogs
clown wig
cocktail dress
conductor cap
Confederate officer hat
Confederate soldier hat
cowboy boots
cowboy hat
crop pants
cross trainers
crown
cutoffs
Davy Crocket/coonskin cap
deerstalker (Sherlock Holmes)
hat
dirndl dress
doughboy helmet
down jacket
dress
dress shoes
drum major hat
Egyptian tiara
elf hat
engineer cap
executioner's hood
feather headdress
fedora
figure skates

fire helmet
flip flops
football helmet
football cleats
galoshes
gangster hat
garrison cap
ghillie suit
golf shoes
gym suit
habit
halo
hard hat
headband
heels
high tops
hiking boots
homburg hat
hood
hoodie
hot pants
jacket
jazz oxfords
jeans
jean jacket
jester hat
jumper
kimono
knight's helmet
knitted cap
laurel wreath
lederhosen
leggings
little black dress
loafers

Mandarin hat
Marine cap
Mary Jane shoes
matador hat
military cap
miner hat
mob cap
moccasins
Mounties' hat
newsboy cap
night cap
nurse's cap
padre hat
painter's cap
pajamas
parka
pedal pushers
peep toe pumps
Pharaoh headpiece
Pilgrim bonnet
pillbox hat
pilot cap
pirate hat
pirate bandana
pith (safari) helmet
pointe shoes
pointy princess hat
policeman's hat
pork pie hat
priest hat
pumps
Puritan man hat
Puritan woman's headpiece
raincoat
Renaissance lady's headpiece

riding boots
riding helmet
rollerblades
roller skates
Roman warrior helmet
running shoes
sailor cap (Dixie cup)
sandals
Santa hat
sarong
scarf
Shakespeare hat
shirt
short shorts
shorts
shower cap
ski cap (beanie)
ski mask
sling backs
slippers
snood
sombrero
space helmet
Spanish conquistador helmet
sport coat
leprechaun hat
stilettos
stovepipe hat
straw boater hat
street dance shoes
suit
sunhat
surgeon's cap
suspender dress
suspenders

Swami turban
sweater
swim fins
swimming cap
tank top
tankini
tap shoes
ten-gallon hat
tennis shoes
tiara
top hat
track suit
trainers
trench coat
tricorn
trousers
T-shirt
tunic
turtleneck
Union officer hat
Union soldier hat
Viking helmet
walking shorts
wedges
wimple

Characterization

SPACE PREP	PLAYER PREP	PERFORMANCE
0	2	2-3
MINUTES	MINUTES	MINUTES

PLAYERS

2

Teach and Practice:

Blocking and Conventions

Characterization

Concentration

Creativity

Ensemble Acting

Group Dynamics

Listening and Silence

Non-vocal Communication

Observation

Physical Control

Plot Structure

Spontaneity

EQUIPMENT
None.

Color Me Pink

Directions

- Each player receives a color. If these are only color names, pictures should be available to show the color.
- Players get a few minutes to jot down any associations with this color: personality traits, ways of dressing, relating, and behaving, etc.
- Two at a time, players act out a generic scene (see page 18) while personifying their colors.
- Scenes should last two to three minutes.
- After the scenes are finished, the rest of the group gets the opportunity to guess what colors they might be.

Examples

- One player is olive, and the other is orange. Olive is an outdoorsy, solid sort of person, and very practical. He is writing in his journal. Orange enters the scene, very outgoing and a bit nervous. She cannot seem to sit still, and this annoys olive.
- One player is gray, and the other is white. Gray is an old person, very bent and arthritic. He is timidly feeding the birds in the park. White is a nun, smiling at all she sees. She sits next to gray and helps feed the birds.

Side Coaching

- How would your color talk?
- How would your color dress and move?
- What would your color like to do?

Evaluation/Critique

- How easy was it to guess the color? What helped you?
- Were the personalities of the color ones you might associate with the color?
- Do you think there are several different ways to interpret that color, or has it been fairly stereotyped?

Challenges and Refinements

- Have more than two players.
- Create a longer scene.

Air Force blue
Alice blue
almond
amber
American rose
amethyst
apple green
apricot
aqua
aquamarine
army green
ash gray
baby blue
baby pink
beige
biscuit
black
blue-violet
blue-green
brass
brick red
bronze
brown
burnt orange
burnt sienna
burnt umber
butter
buttercream
candy apple red
caramel
carnelian
carrot orange
cerise
cerulean
charcoal
chartreuse
cherry red
chocolate
copper
cornflower blue

cranberry
crimson
cyan
dark _____ (insert color)
dove gray
ecru
electric blue
emerald
fire engine red
forest green
fuchsia
gold
gray
green
hot pink
ice
ink
iris
ivory
jade
khaki
lapis
lavender
lemon
light _____ (insert color)
lime green
magenta
mahogany
mauve
melon
midnight blue
mint green
navy blue
neon (insert color)
Nile green
ochre
off-white
olive
orange
pale _____ (insert color)

pastel _____ (insert color)
peach
pearl
phthalo blue
phthalo green
pink
pistachio
plum
puce
pumpkin
purple
raspberry
raw sienna
raw umber
red
red-orange
rose
royal blue
ruby
saffron
sage
salmon
sand
scarlet
sienna
sky blue
tan
tangerine
taupe
teal
turquoise
violet
white
yellow
yellow-green
yellow-orange

Characterization

<table>
<tr><td>SPACE PREP
0
MINUTES</td><td>PLAYER PREP
0
MINUTES</td><td>PERFORMANCE
2-3
MINUTES</td></tr>
</table>

PLAYERS

2

Teach and Practice:

Blocking and Conventions

Characterization

Concentration

Creativity

Ensemble Acting

Group Dynamics

Listening and Silence

Non-vocal Communication

Observation

Physical Control

Plot Structure

Spontaneity

EQUIPMENT
None.

Friends Forever

Directions

- Half the group gets positive friend traits, and the other half gets negative friend traits.
- One player from each group goes to the playing area and starts a generic scene (see page 18).
- Each plays his or her particular friend trait.
- The scene lasts for two to three minutes.

Examples

- A is honest. B is whiny. They are at the movies. A really wants to see this film but keeps telling B that this particular director has made several bad films lately. B complains that they should go. A tells B that she doesn't appreciate her negativity. B tells A she feels picked on. They decide to leave and go their separate ways.
- A is curious. B is rude. They are at the zoo. A hears some strange sounds and wants to investigate their origin. B makes rude comments about why A really wants to investigate. When they get to the area, A cannot understand what he's seeing. B keeps insulting him. A tries to understand why B is so rude, and it drives B mad. B tries to strike A.

Side Coaching

- What kind of a person would have your trait? Explore that.
- Don't let your character think of your trait as negative, that's just the way you are. Don't set out to be negative. Just be it.

Evaluation/Critique

- Did the friend traits suggest certain kinds of characters? Could there have been others? Give examples.
- How did the traits contribute to the conflict? The resolution?
- Could the same characters have other traits more positive or negative than these?

Challenges and Refinements

- Give each character more depth by adding a positive or negative quality.
- Using the same traits, play the two characters in a different situation. Switch gender roles, but keep the traits.

Friend Traits

Positive Traits

adventurous

capable

concerned

courageous

creative

curious

easygoing

fashionable

flamboyant

friendly

fun-loving

giving

grounded

hardworking

honest

hopeful

independent

involved

loving

loyal

open

realistic

relaxed

reliable

responsible

risk-taking

sharing

skilled

smart

talented

up-front

Negative Traits

confused

backstabbing

dangerous

dishonest

disloyal

distant

gossipy

grasping

greedy

lazy

loud

mean-spirited

messy

miserly

monopolizing

radical

rude

selfish

sloppy

smelly

snobby

social-climbing

stuck-up

superstitious

talkative

two-faced

unreliable

unhealthy

whiny

wild

Characterization

PLAYERS

2

Teach and Practice:

Blocking and Conventions

Characterization

Concentration

Creativity

Ensemble Acting

Group Dynamics

Listening and Silence

Non-vocal Communication

Observation

Physical Control

Plot Structure

Spontaneity

EQUIPMENT
None.

High Five!

Directions

- Divide the group into pairs.
- Each pair is given six gestures.
- The players take up to one minute to decide who will use which gestures.
- They play a generic scene (see page 18) lasting one to two minutes in which the characters use each of their gestures at least twice in order to define their characters.

Examples

- Character A has wink, nudge, and high five. Character B has cheek kissing, finger snapping, and A-OK. The scene is a job interview in which a smart-alecky applicant tries to buddy up to a vapid interviewer for a job as a bouncer at a nightclub.
- Character A has clenched fist, nod, and slump. Character B has hug, handshake, and frown. The scene is a doctor's office. Character A is a terrified patient waiting to hear the results of some tests. Character B is the doctor trying to soften terrible news.

Side Coaching

- Make sure everyone can see your gesture.
- Boldly use your gesture.
- Act as if this gesture is part of your personality, not something new.

Evaluation/Critique

- Did the gestures seem natural to the chosen characters?
- Did the gestures help to define the characters?
- Did the gestures further non-vocal communication?

Challenges and Refinements

- Use fewer gestures with timid or younger groups.
- Use more gestures for advanced improv students.
- Have more than two players and add time for a longer scene.

A-OK

air kiss

air quotes

applause

bow

cheek kissing

clenched fist

come here

crazy (finger twirl over ears)

cross heart

curtsey

duh!

elbow bump

eye roll

eyebrow lift

finger gun

fist pump

finger snap

fingers crossed

fist bump

frown

hand kissing

hand rubbing

handshake

hang loose

head scratch

headshake "no"

headshake "yes"

high five

hit

hug

knock on wood

kowtow

"L" loser

live long and prosper

muscle flex

nod

nudge

pat

peace

praying hands

push

salute

scowl

shoot self in head

shrug

sign of the cross

slump

smile

take a picture

talk to the hand

thumbing nose

thumbs down

thumbs in ears

thumbs up

time-out

tongue in cheek

tremble

"V" for victory

wave

whatever

wink

z-snap

Characterization

SPACE PREP	PLAYER PREP	PERFORMANCE
0	0	2-3
MINUTES	MINUTES	MINUTES

PLAYERS

2

Teach and Practice:

Blocking and Conventions

Characterization

Concentration

Creativity

Ensemble Acting

Group Dynamics

Listening and Silence

Non-vocal Communication

Observation

Physical Control

Plot Structure

Spontaneity

EQUIPMENT
Assortment of jewelry (optional).

My Tiara

Directions
- Divide the group into pairs.
- Give each player a card with a type of jewelry on it. (Optional: Ask players to bring in objects of their own that are not too valuable.)
- Each character in the pair has to wear the type of jewelry and incorporate it into his or her character.
- Groups perform a two- to three-minute generic scene of their choosing (See page 18 for examples) focusing on how this jewelry enhances their characters.

Examples
- The clothing objects are a tiara and cuff links. Two frightened teenagers at their first dance trying to be cool.
- The clothing objects are a cameo and an earring. An old lady, all dressed up in her finest, is stuck at a wedding party with a young man wearing a dangling earring.

Side Coaching
- Your character has chosen this jewelry because he or she loves it. It defines him or her.
- The jewelry is very meaningful to your character.

Evaluation/Critique
- Were the pieces of jewelry incorporated into a believable character?
- Did the jewelry define the characters?
- Were the characters realistic or stereotypical?

Challenges and Refinements
- Play the scenes for broad stereotypes based on the type of jewelry.
- Play the scenes for subtlety and realism.

Jewelry and Accessories

ankle bracelet

barrette

belt

belt buckle

bolo tie

bonnet

bow tie

bracelet

bracelet, large diamonds

bracelet, large emeralds

brightly beaded necklace

brooch

cameo

cap

class ring

coin purse

cuff links

diamond cocktail ring

earring, diamond stud

earring, long dangly

engagement ring

eyebrow ring

gloves

hair clip

handbag

handkerchief

hat

hat pin

headband

Hello Kitty pin

locket

massive gold neck chain

military medals

necklace

necklace of feathers

nose ring

pendant

pillbox hat

pin with peace symbol

pink bow hair band

promise ring

rhinestone-encrusted
   eyeglasses

ring

"rubber ducky" earrings

scarf

scarf pin

shawl

shoe buckles

simple choker necklace

simple gold band ring

single black pearl earrings

snuffbox

Native American symbols

Super Bowl ring

tiara

tie

tie clip

tie tack

toe ring

tongue piercing

university ring

wallet

watch, pendant

watch, pin

watch, pocket

watch, wrist

zipper pull with diamonds

Characterization

PLAYERS

4

Teach and Practice:

Blocking and Conventions

Characterization

Concentration

Creativity

Ensemble Acting

Group Dynamics

Listening and Silence

Non-vocal Communication

Observation

Physical Control

Plot Structure

Spontaneity

EQUIPMENT
None.

Please and Thank You

Directions

- Divide into groups of four.
- Two players are the parents, and two are the children.
- The parents each get a manners card. This "good manners" attribute is very important to them.
- The scene is a dinner table conversation.
- The players get one minute to plan their scene.
- The conversation starts, and the parents play their "good manners" card to the hilt.

Examples

- Parents have "don't talk about yourself" and "don't stare." The scene starts as the kids talk about school very enthusiastically, but they are constantly reminded that "it's not nice to talk about yourself." As they become baffled and stare at the parents or each other, they keep getting reminded not to stare.
- Parents have "smile" and "sit with good posture." The scene starts as one child is complaining about the other. A parent tells him or her to smile. The other is slumping and is told to sit up straight. These repeated admonitions annoy the kids.

Evaluation/Critique

- Did the "manners" help or hurt the family communication and/or relationships?
- Were the kids' responses positive or negative?
- Did the admonitions lead to conflict?
- How was the conflict resolved?

Manners

Act dignified.

Be helpful.

Be honest.

Be kind.

Be positive.

Be punctual.

Be respectful.

Be thoughtful.

Clean up after yourself.

Don't ask personal questions.

Don't be selfish.

Don't brag.

Don't bully or associate with bullies.

Don't call attention to yourself.

Don't cheat.

Don't crack knuckles.

Don't cut in line.

Don't dominate conversations.

Don't grab.

Don't interrupt.

Don't leave the table while eating.

Don't make a scene or call attention to self.

Don't point.

Don't pry.

Don't push or shove.

Don't put others down.

Don't speak in anger.

Don't stare.

Don't take more than your fair share.

Don't talk about yourself.

Don't talk too loudly.

Don't talk with food in your mouth.

Don't throw things.

Dress appropriately.

Eat only after host has started.

Eat quietly.

Follow the rules.

Help others in need.

Keep away from bad company.

Knock on doors; don't barge in.

Mind your own business.

Mind your parents.

Never assume anything about anyone.

Never cut others down.

Never talk about money.

Never talk badly about another's religion.

Relax.

Remember peoples' names.

Report crimes.

Respect boundaries.

Say "excuse me."

Sit with good posture.

Smile.

Speak properly and clearly.

Speak the truth.

Take small bites.

Telephone before visiting people.

Thank others.

Think of others first.

Wait your turn.

Wash your hands.

Characterization

PLAYERS

2

Teach and Practice:

Blocking and Conventions

Characterization

Concentration

Creativity

Ensemble Acting

Group Dynamics

Listening and Silence

Non-vocal Communication

Observation

Physical Control

Plot Structure

Spontaneity

EQUIPMENT
None.

In the Mood

Directions

- Divide the group into pairs.
- Each player in the pair draws a mood.
- The scene is about two friends who are trying to decide what to do over the weekend.
- The players act in their respective moods, which complicates the choices for weekend activities.
- The scene starts immediately and ends when the decision is finally resolved.

Examples

- One player is lonely, and the other is mischievous. The mischievous one wants to go out late on Saturday night and toilet paper a friend's house. The lonely one opposes this because he doesn't want to alienate the friend.
- One player is drained, and the other is sad. They go through a variety of ideas for activities, but none satisfy either one because they are both so low.

Side Coaching

- Introduce your mood early.
- Emphasize your mood. Let it be bigger than life.
- Let your mood be part of who you are in the moment.

Evaluation/Critique

- How did the moods affect the suggestions for activities?
- How did the players show the moods?
- How did the moods affect the outcome of the decision?
- Were the moods shown non-vocally as well as vocally?

Challenges and Refinements

- In the middle of the scene, have the players switch their moods.
- Exaggerate the moods.

accepted

accomplished

aggravated

alone

amused

angry

animated

annoyed

anxious

apathetic

ashamed

awake

aware

bewildered

blissful

bored

calm

caring

cheerful

chipper

cold

complacent

confused

contented

cranky

crushed

cynical

depressed

determined

devious

disappointed

discontented

ditzy

drained

ecstatic

energetic

enraged

enthralled

envious

excited

exhausted

flirty

foul

frustrated

giddy

giggly

gloomy

grateful

groggy

happy

hopeful

hyper

impressed

indifferent

infuriated

irate

irrational

irritated

jealous

jubilant

lethargic

lonely

loved

melancholic

mellow

mischievous

moody

optimistic

peaceful

pessimistic

pleased

rejected

rejuvenated

relaxed

relieved

replenished

restless

rushed

sad

satisfied

shocked

silly

sleepy

stressed

surprised

sympathetic

thankful

tired

touched

uncomfortable

weird

SPACE PREP	PLAYER PREP	PERFORMANCE
0	**2**	**2-3**
MINUTES	MINUTES	MINUTES

PLAYERS

2

Teach and Practice:

Blocking and Conventions

Characterization

Concentration

Creativity

Ensemble Acting

Group Dynamics

Listening and Silence

Non-vocal Communication

Observation

Physical Control

Plot Structure

Spontaneity

EQUIPMENT
None.

Phobia Game

Directions

- Divide group into pairs, preferably one male and one female.
- The scene is a blind date or a generic scene from page 18.
- Each player draws a phobia.
- After two minutes of preparation, they play a scene in which their phobias come into full force.

Examples

- A has a fear of garlic, and B has a fear of imperfection. A comes tentatively to B's door to meet her for a date. He does not want to get too close in case she smells of garlic. B is fussing around inside, fearful that she will not be good enough. When A seems reluctant at the door, she assumes that it is all her fault because she is just not perfect. She refuses to go out on the date.
- A has a fear of books, and B has a fear of making decisions. A enters B's house only to find her reading a book. B cannot understand why A is acting so strangely. She doesn't know what to do and tries all sorts of things. A suggests they leave right away to go to a movie. B isn't sure if she wants to go. A suggests a concert while gradually edging to the door and fleeing.

Side Coaching

- Your phobia is part of your personality. It's nothing new; it's just you.
- Don't forget to respond to your partner's phobia. Since it's not yours, you think it's unusual.
- Go ahead and make assumptions about your partner — even if they're unfounded.

Evaluation/Critique

- Did the phobia seem hidden or obvious?
- Did it develop/escalate throughout the scene?
- Did the phobia determine the plot/conflict? Did it drive the scene?
- Was there another way to have played the phobia?

Challenges and Refinements

- Have the players try to hide their phobias.
- Perform a scene in which the character conquers his or her phobia.

Phobias

ablutophobia — fear of bathing, washing, or cleaning

achluophobia — fear of the dark

acousticophobia — fear of sounds, including your own voice

acrophobia — fear of heights

agoraphobia — fear of places or events where escape is impossible or help is unavailable

agyrophobia — fear of crossing roads

aichmophobia — fear of sharp or pointed objects, such as a needle or a pointing finger

ailurophobia — fear of cats

androphobia — fear of men

anthophobia — fear of flowers

anthropophobia — fear of people or being in a group

apiphobia — fear of bees

aquaphobia — fear of water

arachnophobia — fear of spiders and other arachnids

atychiphobia — fear of failure

autophobia — fear of loneliness or being alone

aviophobia — fear of flying

bacillophobia (or bacteriophobia) — fear of microbes, germs

ballistophobia — fear of missiles or bullets

barophobia — fear of gravity

bathophobia — fear of depths

batonophobia — fear of plants

batophobia — fear of heights or being close to high buildings

batrachophobia — fear of amphibians, such as frogs, toads, newts, salamanders

belonephobia — fear of sharp objects, especially needles

bibliophobia — fear of books

blennophobia — fear of slime

bogyphobia — fear of bogies or the bogeyman

bovinophobia — fear of cattle

bromidrophobia — fear of body odors

brontophobia — fear of thunder and lightning

bufonophobia — fear of toads

cacophobia — fear of ugliness

cainophobia (or cainotophobia) — fear of newness, novelty

caligynephobia — fear of beautiful women

cancerophobia — fear of developing a cancerous growth

cardiophobia — fear of the heart or heart disease

carnophobia — fear of meat

catagelophobia — fear of being ridiculed

catapedaphobia — fear of jumping from high and low places

cathisophobia — fear of sitting down

catoptrophobia — fear of mirrors

cenophobia — fear of void or open spaces

centophobia — fear of new things or ideas

Phobias

cetaphobia — fear of whales

chaetophobia — fear of hair

cheimaphobia (or cheimatophobia) — fear of cold

chemophobia — fear of chemicals or working with chemicals

cherophobia — fear of gaiety or happiness

chiroptophobia — fear of bats

claustrophobia — fear of having no escape and being closed in small spaces

coulrophobia — fear of clowns

cynophobia — fear of dogs

decidophobia — fear of making decisions

dentophobia (or odontophobia) — fear of dentists and dental procedures

disposophobia — fear of getting rid of things

ebulliophobia — fear of bubbles

emetophobia — fear of vomiting

enetophobia — fear of vaccines or vaccinations

entomophobia — fear of insects

equinophobia — fear of horses

ergophobia (or ergasiophobia) — fear of work

erythrophobia — fear of blushing

friggatriskaidekaphobia — fear of Friday the 13th

gelotophobia — fear of being laughed at

gephyrophobia — fear of bridges

gerascophobia — fear of growing old or aging

glossophobia — fear of speaking in public

gurgephobia — fear of the abyss, particularly the ocean floor or outer space

gymnophobia — fear of nudity

gynophobia — fear of women

halitophobia — fear of bad breath

haptephobia — fear of being touched

heliophobia — fear of sunlight

hemophobia (or haemophobia) — fear of blood

herpetophobia — fear of reptiles or amphibians

hexakosioihexekontahexaphobia — fear of the number 666

homophobia — fear of homosexuals

hoplophobia — fear of firearms

hylophobia — fear of trees, forests, or wood

ichthyophobia — fear of fish

kainolophobia (or kainophobia) — fear of anything new or novel

ligyrophobia — fear of loud noises

lipophobia — fear of fats in food

lygophobia — fear of night or darkness

mottephobia — fear of butterflies or moths

murophobia — fear of mice or rats

mysophobia — fear of contamination or germs

necrophobia — fear of death or dead things

negrophobia — fear of black people

neophobia — fear of new things or experiences

nomophobia — fear of being out of mobile phone contact

nosocomephobia — fear of hospitals

nosophobia — fear of contracting a disease

nyctophobia — fear of darkness

oikophobia — fear of home surroundings or the familiar

olfactophobia — fear of odors or smells

ophidiophobia — fear of snakes

ordacleaphobia — fear of imperfection

ornithophobia — fear of birds

osmophobia — fear of odors

panphobia — fear of everything, or fear of an unknown cause

paraskevidekatriaphobia — fear of Friday the 13th

pediophobia — fear of dolls

phagophobia — fear of swallowing

pharmacophobia — fear of medication

phasmophobia — fear of ghosts and phantoms

philophobia — fear of being in love or falling in love

phobophobia — fear of having a phobia

phonophobia — fear of loud sounds

porphyrophobia — fear of the color purple

pyrophobia — fear of fire or flames

radiophobia — fear of radioactivity or x-rays

scoleciphobia — fear of worms

scolionophobia — fear of school

scopophobia — fear of being stared at

scotophobia — fear of darkness

selachophobia — fear of sharks

sichuaphobia — fear of Chinese food

sociophobia — fear of social gatherings or interactions

somniphobia — fear of sleep

taphophobia — fear of the grave or being buried alive

technophobia — fear of technology

telephonophobia (or telephobia) — fear of making or taking phone calls

tetraphobia — fear of the number four

thanatophobia — fear of being dead or dying

tokophobia — fear of childbirth or pregnancy

traumatophobia — fear of having an injury

trichophobia — fear of the sight of loose hairs

triskaidekaphobia (or terdekaphobia) — fear of the number thirteen

trypanophobia — fear of needles

workplace phobia — fear of the workplace

xenophobia — fear of the foreign or strange

zoophobia — fear of animals

Characterization

SPACE PREP
0
MINUTES

PLAYER PREP
1
MINUTES

PERFORMANCE
2-3
MINUTES

PLAYERS

2

Teach and Practice:

Blocking and Conventions

Characterization

Concentration

Creativity

Ensemble Acting

Group Dynamics

Listening and Silence

Non-vocal Communication

Observation

Physical Control

Plot Structure

Spontaneity

EQUIPMENT
None.

Relationship Dyads

Directions

- Divide into pairs.
- Each pair draws a relationship.
- They get one minute to prepare a scene in which they interact.
- The scene will last two to three minutes.

Examples

- Employer/employee: The employer has to tell the employee that she is being fired.
- Homeless person/passerby: The homeless person really annoys the passerby for money until the passerby throws a quarter at him.
- Bully/victim: The victim stands up to the bully.

Side Coaching

- Make your character and relationship clear from the start.
- Does the relationship define your character?
- Use speech to help define your relationship.
- Use movement to help define your relationship.
- Let us see how you feel about your relationship.

Evaluation/Critique

- How did the players portray their characters?
- Were the characters broad stereotypes or more subtle?
- What made each character unique?
- Did the players rely on specific aspects of character, such as vocalizations, gestures, facial expressions, walks?

Challenges and Refinements

- Switch roles.
- Switch status.
- Exaggerate.

Relationships

airline ticket seller/frequent flyer

artist/subject

aunt/uncle

babysitter/child

babysitter/parent

boyfriend/girlfriend

brother/brother

brother/sister

bully/victim

coworkers

colleagues

cousins

customer/clerk

doctor/patient

employer/employee

film director/star

friend/enemy

Good Samarian/victim

gossip/person gossiped about

homeless person/passerby

invalid/doctor

lawyer/client

lifeguard/swimmer

lonely unmarried person/happy single person

married couple

martial arts instructor/student

mistress/someone else's husband

nosy busybody

parent/child

pilot/passenger

priest/parishioner

professor/student

school principal/teacher

sick person/doctor

significant others

single dad/child

single man/single woman

single mom/child

sister/sister

soul mates

star/fan

state governor/environmental activist

strangers thrown together in a crisis

tax collector/tax avoider

teacher/student

telephone repairman/homeowner

two lonely people at a 24-hour diner

worker/foreman

Characterization

SPACE PREP	PLAYER PREP	PERFORMANCE
0	**2**	**3-5**
MINUTES	MINUTES	MINUTES

PLAYERS

2+

Teach and Practice:

Blocking and Conventions

Characterization

Concentration

Creativity

Ensemble Acting

Group Dynamics

Listening and Silence

Non-vocal Communication

Observation

Physical Control

Plot Structure

Spontaneity

EQUIPMENT

None.

Skillful

Directions

- Each player receives a skill that they keep to themselves.
- Players get a minute to jot down associations with types of characters who might have that skill.
- The director creates a type of scene in which a decision has to be made, like how to get out of some kind of crisis perhaps. (See the "Enclosed Spaces" list on page 88 for places in which players can be trapped.)
- Starting with two players, they try to solve this problem using their skills. These have to be plausible: A speed reader cannot read her way out of a burning building, but she might be able to read and remember instructions taped to the wall.
- Others may join in until the crisis is resolved.

Examples

- A can sew beautifully, and B can stay positive. The crisis is being trapped on the roof of a burning building. A looks around for pieces of material from which to fashion a rope while B urges him on.
- A can relate to children, and B can run very quickly. The crisis is being trapped in an elevator. (Note: There are no children, and there is no place to run.) Perhaps A has a very understanding, calming presence because of his skill. B's skill makes her a go-getter but very competitive — she always wants to do something! A helps her focus, and she figures out how to climb through the roof of the elevator to get help.

Side Coaching

- Show, don't tell.

Evaluation/Critique

- Were the skills shown or told?
- Did the skills determine the action?
- Were the characters subtle or more stereotyped?
- Did the characters have nuances?
- Were the characters able to creatively problem-solve using their skills, or did the skills show different useful personality traits?
- Were they believable?

Challenges and Refinements

- Exaggerate the skills.
- Make the skill a super power.

balance on thin places

be a respected leader

calm people down

cook creatively

drive a sports car

do acrobatics

do complex equations

do crossword or sudoku puzzles

do mental math

doodle

draw well

handle a motorcycle

imitate accents

inspire people

interior design

interpret dreams

juggle

leap far distances

lift heavy objects

make people feel at ease

multitasking

organize events

play several instruments

relate to animals

relate to children

remember life events clearly

remember many facts

run for long periods of time

run very quickly

sew beautifully

sing on pitch

speak many languages

speed read

stay calm in a crisis

stay positive

take huge risks fearlessly

think quickly on your feet

tolerate loud noises

train animals

write music

write novels

write poetry

Enclosed Spaces

abandoned refrigerator

air vent

alley

attic

bank vault

baseball dugout

basement

bathroom stall

bathtub

box

broom closet

cabin

car trunk

catacomb

cave

chemistry lab

closet

clothes dryer

coffin

computer lab

confessional booth

construction site

costume storage area

crawl space

crypt

CT scanner

darkroom

doctor's examination room

doghouse

dressing room

duffle bag

dumbwaiter

Dumpster

elevator

empty swimming pool

Ferris wheel

fruit cellar

fun house

garage

glass elevator

gondola

grandfather clock

greenhouse

hollow log

hotel room

ice cream truck

jail cell

laboratory

laundry chute

locker

luggage

mad scientist's lab

mausoleum

meat locker

moving van

Murphy bed

office cubicle

packing trunk

phone booth

photo booth

portable toilet

projection booth

recording studio

revolving door

sculptor's studio

secret passageway

sewer

shower stall

sleeping bag

storage room

storage shed

storm cellar

subway car

suitcase

swimming pool filter room

tent

theatre box seat

theatre lighting booth

tool shed

trash can

trash compactor

tunnel

tunnel of love

walk-in freezer

well

zoo cage

Valley Girls vs. Snobs

Characterization

SPACE PREP
0
MINUTES

PLAYER PREP
0
MINUTES

PERFORMANCE
3-4
MINUTES

PLAYERS
2+

Directions

- Each player draws or is given a stereotype that they keep to themselves.
- The director suggests a type of scene that could involve several players. (For example: on the playground, at the bus stop, on a school bus, in the classroom, at a museum, at the park, at the zoo, or see page 18 for more generic scenes.)
- The director chooses one player at random who starts a scene. One at a time, other players enter.
- They play their stereotype to the hilt as the scene continues.
- The scene lasts three to four minutes.

Example

Player 1 as Eeyore is a school bus driver. He starts his bus route complaining softly to himself. Even before he picks up his first passenger, he lets us know how much he dislikes kids. Player 2, a do-gooder, gets on the bus, all sunshine and good cheer, trying to cheer up the driver. Later, Player 3, the bully, gets in and makes a nasty comment to both the do-gooder and the Eeyore. Player 4, the know-it-all, gets on and tries to analyze why they are all so upset. The bully beats him up, the do-gooder tries to stop him but gets hurt, and the driver looks at the audience as if to say, "I told you so!"

Side Coaching

- Be broad from the beginning. Go for it!

Evaluation/Critique

- Does the stereotype determine such things as walk, facial expression, ways of speaking, and actions?
- Does the stereotype further the action? Lead to conflict? Resolve it?
- Could the stereotype be a real person? What could have led to this trait being predominant?

Challenges and Refinements

- Choose just one stereotype and have two characters with the same stereotype play a scene.
- Go back into the character's past and design a "The making of a _____" scene.

Teach and Practice:

Blocking and Conventions

Characterization

Concentration

Creativity

Ensemble Acting

Group Dynamics

Listening and Silence

Non-vocal Communication

Observation

Physical Control

Plot Structure

Spontaneity

EQUIPMENT
None.

Stereotypes

accommodator
achiever
adventurer
airhead
bad sport
bleeding heart
boor
bore
braggart
bully
company man (or woman)
complainer
conformist
creep
critic
culture vulture
cutter
daydreamer
delinquent
do-gooder
doomsayer
doormat
downer
Eeyore
enthusiast
entrepreneur
envier
evangelist
fantasist
flirt
follower
free spirit
giggler

glutton
goody-goody
gossip
grabber
groupie
hermit
hypochondriac
innocent
interpreter
isolationist
joker
killjoy
kiss-up
klutz
know-it-all
latecomer
loner
loser
manipulator
meddler
miser
missionary
nag
narcissist
nay-sayer
nurturer
optimist
perfectionist
performer
Pollyanna
poor me
practical joker
procrastinator

rebel
risk-taker
romantic
rubber-necker
rule follower
saboteur
sadist
scaredy cat
scene stealer
Scrooge
sexist pig
show-off
sissy
skeptic
slob
smug one
sneak
social climber
social snob
sore loser
teacher's pet
thinker
true believer
user
valley girl
victim
visionary
wannabe
whiner
worrywart
xenophobe
zealot

It's My Name!

Directions

- Divide into pairs.
- Each player draws an unusual name.
- In pairs, players improvise a generic scene (a random meeting at a bus stop, sitting next to each other at a film, or see page 18) in which they focus on how their name has shaped who they are.
- Play the stereotype.

Examples

- Robin Banks meets Crystal Glass at a bus stop. Crystal is beautiful and delicate, and Robin wants to impress her with his macho ways. Eventually, he starts to brag about his career as a bank robber.
- Owen Money meets Luke Warm at a table in a restaurant where they have to sit at the same table. Owen starts his sob story about his unfortunate financial situation. Luke tries to be polite but becomes more and more annoyed and then tries to ignore him.

Evaluation/Critique

- Did the names determine the character? In what ways?
- In what other ways were these characters developed? Did they have specific ways of speaking, gesturing, and relating?

Challenges and Refinements

- Have the group make up their own names or even use names they know from literature. (Charles Dickens, Oscar Wilde, and other British writers have characters with marvelous names, though not real.) For example, what would a modern day Prospero or Iago be like if they lived up to their names?

Be sensitive. If you have people in your group with strange names, don't play this! Be careful. If you look up weird names, be sure to sound them out first. A good number of them are X-rated.

Characterization

SPACE PREP	PLAYER PREP	PERFORMANCE
0 MINUTES	0 MINUTES	3-4 MINUTES

PLAYERS
2

Teach and Practice:

Blocking and Conventions
Characterization
Concentration
Creativity
Ensemble Acting
Group Dynamics
Listening and Silence
Non-vocal Communication
Observation
Physical Control
Plot Structure
Spontaneity

EQUIPMENT
None.

Unusual Names

Andy Mann	Harry Hiney	Rhoda Rage
Anna Prentice	Hazel Nutt	Rick O'Shea
Anna Sassin	Holly Bush	Robin Banks
Annette Curtain	Honey Pye	Robin Plunder
Artie Choke	Ima Hogg	Rocky Stone
Barb Dwyer	Jay Bird	Rose Bush
Brandy Bottle	Justin Case	Rosemary Plant
Carrie Oakey	Justine Time	Rosie Peach
Crystal Glass	Louden Clear	Russell Sprout
Daisy Picking	Luke Warm	Rusty Nails
Dan Druff	Marj Oram	Sandy Shore
Dee Zaster	Nick Cut	Seymour Legg
Doug Graves	Onya Bike	Shandy Lear
Dusty Rhodes	Owen Money	Stan Still
Dwayne Pipe	Paige Turner	Ted E. Bayer
Emerald Stone	Pearl E. Whites	Terri Bull
Eva Sigh	Penny Whistle	Tim Burr
Gayle Storm	Penny Wise	Warren Peace
Harley Davidson	Pete Sake	

Job Interview

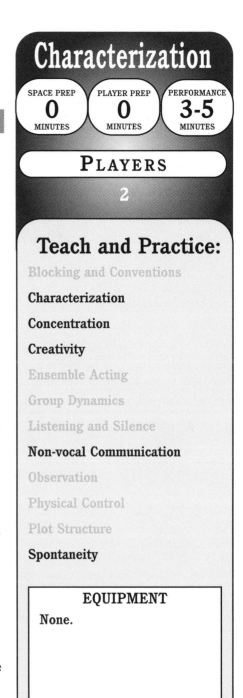

Characterization

SPACE PREP	PLAYER PREP	PERFORMANCE
0	0	3-5
MINUTES	MINUTES	MINUTES

PLAYERS

2

Directions

- Divide into pairs.
- One person is the interviewer, and the other is the interviewee for a job.
- The interviewee in each pair receives an imaginary or unusual occupation.
- The interviewer does not know what the interviewee's current occupation is, only that he or she has been told that the person might be useful to the organization.
- The scene progresses as the interviewer tries to discover the occupation, and the interviewee tries to show his or her enthusiasm for it by developing his or her character.

Examples

- A jester is interviewed for a job, and through good-natured joking around, he tries to show the interviewer how taking himself lightly would help his reputation as a manager.
- A shadow is being interviewed and tries to show the interviewer how important it is to have someone around to witness what she does so she will never feel alone.

Side Coaching

- Interviewee — Emphasize your skills without openly stating them.
- Interviewer — Listen carefully for hints and go with them. The interviewee will let you know when you're right.

Evaluation/Critique

- How did the interviewee reveal his or her occupation?
- How did the interviewer discover the occupation?
- How did the interviewer react to the occupation?
- Once the occupation was known, did it affect their previous relationship?
- Did the interviewee manage to convince the interviewer that he or she would be an asset? If so, how? If not, why not?
- Did the occupation determine how the interviewee behaved? Did the character seem to fit the occupation?

Challenges and Refinements

- The interviewer is told that he or she should or should not hire this person.
- The interviewee is told he or she wants or does not want this job.

Teach and Practice:

Blocking and Conventions

Characterization

Concentration

Creativity

Ensemble Acting

Group Dynamics

Listening and Silence

Non-vocal Communication

Observation

Physical Control

Plot Structure

Spontaneity

EQUIPMENT

None.

Unusual Occupations

aura cleanser

bed warmer

bibliotherapist

body double

brow mopper

BS detector

bully immobilizer

card reader

cat tamer

cheerer-upper

conscience

danger sniffer

dresser

Elvis impersonator

fan bearer

fashion advisor

fashion police

flatterer

food eater

food taster

fortune teller

gesture interpreter

ghost buster

gift picker

greeting card writer

guru

hired friend

hired stalker

imaginary servant

improvised songwriter

jail breaker

jester

jingle composer

joke interpreter

lemonade maker

lock picker

mind reader

mindfulness teacher

neutral witness

paint scraper

personal cheerleader

personal mime

personal psychic

personal scribe

personal worrier

pet therapist

pie thrower

pillow fluffer

professional flirt

punster

puppet maker

rioter

shadow

soother

surrogate pet for a day

tea leaf reader

tire washer

town crier

town lunatic

trumpeter

truth teller

verbal Valentine deliverer

Devil Made Me Do It

Directions

- Divide the group into pairs.
- Each player receives a vice on a card. This vice is kept secret from the other player and becomes the player's motivation for acting.
- The scene is a taxi cab. One player is the driver, and the other is the passenger.
- The scene starts, and the characters begin a discussion in which their vices become more and more predominant.

Examples

- A is cruel, and B is vain. A, the driver, acts mockingly nice to middle-aged woman B. He has just picked her up at a salon. B is very proud of her new look and talks about how happy the hairdresser was with it. A becomes more and more cruel to her as he ramps up the backhanded compliments. B gets very upset but continues to justify herself by praising all aspects of her life.
- A is a procrastinator, and B is malicious. A picks B up at a show, and B asks to go to a well-known hotel. A is garrulous and doesn't seem to know the way. B criticizes her driving, her sense of direction, the way she speaks English, and eventually her cultural/social background. As a result, A gets "lost" in the city.

Side Coaching

- Start by choosing one trait of your vice and emphasizing it.
- Leave room in the beginning to let your vice build.
- Listen to your partner for clues as to how you can interact.

Evaluation/Critique

- Did the vices actually escalate?
- What happened when they did?
- Did the vices lead to conflicts? How?
- What might have happened if the scene had gone on?

Challenges and Refinements

- Switch characters, but keep the same vice.
- Switch vices, but keep the same characters.
- Have one character with the opposite of their vice. (The vain person is very self-deprecating, etc.)

Characterization

SPACE PREP	PLAYER PREP	PERFORMANCE
0 MINUTES	0 MINUTES	2-3 MINUTES

PLAYERS

2

Teach and Practice:

Blocking and Conventions

Characterization

Concentration

Creativity

Ensemble Acting

Group Dynamics

Listening and Silence

Non-vocal Communication

Observation

Physical Control

Plot Structure

Spontaneity

EQUIPMENT
None.

Vices

amoral

angry

apathetic

arrogant

bamboozling

boastful

cheater

cold

complaining

coveting

crafty

critical

cruel

deceitful

disinterested

disloyal

embezzler

envious

fearful

gluttonous

gossipy

greedy

immoral

impatient

inflexible

jealous

lazy

loudmouthed

lustful

lying

malicious

mean-spirited

melancholic

nagging

pessimistic

prideful

procrastinating

selfish

shameless

skinflint

slanderous

sloppy

slothful

slovenly

two-faced

unaware

unfair

ungrateful

unkind

vain

weak

wishy-washy

Virtuous Family

Directions

- Divide into groups of four.
- Take a minute to decide who will have which role in a family. (Parent, sibling, etc.)
- Each player draws a virtue that is kept secret from the rest.
- Each player is to play his or her virtue to see how the scene of a family sitting at a dinner table evolves.
- The scene lasts two to three minutes.

Example

The father is thoughtful, the mother is generous, the son is humble, and the daughter is confident. The scene starts with the daughter talking about her successes at school, not bragging, of course. The father really thinks about these and makes relevant comments. The mother praises her. The son does too, but when asked about his own substantial achievements, he tries to slightly downplay them.

Side Coaching

- Focus on one or two aspects of your virtue to start, and really play it.
- Give others time to display their virtues as you build your own.
- It's OK if you can't figure out the other virtues right away. Just keep responding as it seems appropriate.

Evaluation/Critique

- Were the virtues obvious?
- How were they incorporated into the characters?
- Did the virtues contribute to any kind of conflict? If so, how? If not, why not?
- Did the virtues suggest any particular types of characters?

Challenges and Refinements

- Exaggerate the virtues to make stereotyped characters. How does this change the scene?
- Switch virtues with another character in the scene, but maintain the same plot.
- Play the opposite of your virtue. For example, the humble son becomes a braggart; the thoughtful father becomes thoughtless, etc. How does this change the scene?

Teach and Practice:

Blocking and Conventions

Characterization

Concentration

Creativity

Ensemble Acting

Group Dynamics

Listening and Silence

Non-vocal Communication

Observation

Physical Control

Plot Structure

Spontaneity

EQUIPMENT
None.

Virtues

Traditional Virtues

clean

committed

compassionate

confident

conscientious

considerate

cooperative

courageous

courteous

creative

curious

dependable

determined

dignified

disciplined

fair

frugal

generous

grateful

helpful

honest

hopeful

hospitable

humble

humorous

impartial

industrious

intuitive

merciful

open

optimistic

patient

perseverant

prudent

respectful

Roman Virtues

spiritual authority

stable

strong

temperate

tenacious

thoughtful

trustworthy

truthful

understanding

wholesome

wise

witty

Trapped with a Libra

Directions

- Divide the group into pairs.
- Each member of the pair gets a different Western astrological type.
- Pairs get one minute to plan a scene in which they are trapped and must use their astrological traits to get out of the trap. (See the list of "Enclosed Spaces" on page 88.)
- Each scene has a beginning, middle, and an ending.

Examples

- Pisces and Leo are trapped in a cave. The scene starts as Leo compels Pisces to enter the cave against her wishes. She enters though, because she says she senses that Leo really needs to do this. Leo calms her down. Then, rocks fall and they are trapped in the cave. Leo is not bothered and starts to scout out alternative ways to escape. Pisces volunteers to scout up ahead. A scream is heard as Pisces disappears into a pit.
- Virgo and Scorpio are trapped in an elevator. Virgo enters carrying a briefcase and papers, reviewing some papers. Scorpio enters and flirts with Virgo, who is very disapproving. The elevator stalls. Virgo is annoyed by Scorpio who moves in on Virgo, telling her to remain calm. Virgo slaps Scorpio as the elevator starts back up.

Side Coaching

- Show, don't tell your trait.
- Be as creative as you can with your trait.
- Expand on the few words of your trait to come up with your solutions.

Evaluation/Critique

- Were there clearly differentiated characters?
- Did the characters' personalities motivate the conflict, the resolution, or both?
- Was there a clear beginning, middle, and ending?

Challenges and Refinements

- Choose one of the astrological types to "solve" the problem before the scene starts.
- Make one type an introvert and the other an extrovert.

Teach and Practice:

Blocking and Conventions

Characterization

Concentration

Creativity

Ensemble Acting

Group Dynamics

Listening and Silence

Non-vocal Communication

Observation

Physical Control

Plot Structure

Spontaneity

EQUIPMENT
None.

Western Astrological Types

Capricorn (December 22-January 19)
Responsible, detail-oriented, likes tangible results, precise, persevering, practical, clear-minded, dutiful.

Aquarius (January 20-February 18)
Independent, clever, objective, original, aloof, noncommittal, reserved, likes variety.

Pisces (February 19-March 20)
Intuitive, flexible, self-sacrificing, insightful, wise, empathetic, devoted.

Aries (March 21-April 20)
Resilient, energetic, spontaneous, impulsive, direct, easygoing, independent, arbitrary, optimistic, risk-taker, wants his or her own way.

Taurus (April 21-May 21)
Practical, decisive, dependable, persevering, concrete thinker, faithful, ender, stubborn, can be hot-tempered when really pushed.

Gemini (May 22-June 21)
Versatile, happy, curious, talkative, clever, critical thinker, precise, quick-witted, social, restless.

Cancer (June 22-July 23)
Romantic, caring, feeling, empathetic, home-loving, sensitive, impressionable, naïve, trusting, affectionate.

Leo (July 24-August 23)
Decisive, risk-taking, calm, self-reliant, intelligent, strong convictions, self confident, passionate.

Virgo (August 24-September 23)
Orderly, reliable, critical thinker, pragmatic, good with details, cautious, reserved, faithful.

Libra (September 24-October 23)
Creative, impulsive, needs harmony and beauty, enterprising, tactful, sociable, needs freedom.

Scorpio (October 24-November 22)
Uncompromising, provocative, strong-willed, cynical, enormous emotional strength, access to dark powers.

Sagittarius (November 23-December 21)
An achiever, strong convictions, highly educated, has far-reaching plans, enthusiastic, enjoys partnerships, loves travel.

Narrative/Plot

Narrative is essentially telling a story. It is what happens. Of course, the narrative involves characters as well as plot, but in this section we focus primarily on the development of the story's plot elements. Traditionally, a story has a beginning, a middle, and an ending. In between, there are usually conflicts leading to a climax or two, and in the end, there is usually a satisfying conclusion to the action. Along the way, there may be foreshadowing of events to come. They may be signposted to create suspense or even to trick the audience, if that was the intent, as it might be if the plot were a mystery. Of course, the type of story to be told is always a consideration since there are different conventions in different genres. Sometimes you want to stick to these expectations, and sometimes you may prefer to veer off the tried-and-true trail to come up with something new. Usually, the progression of the story is linear. In other words, there is a logical progression of events often sequenced in a timeline that goes from the beginning to the end, which occurs later or in the future. However, it is sometimes fun to play with time, as in the case with a structure from future back to past or the use of flashbacks.

Narratives can be built around events, characters, or places. The who, what, why, when, and how of a story structure may be important to keep in mind, especially in longer narratives. Most of these activities are short, and many focus on the process of building particular aspects of plot rather than a polished and finished product. So have fun and enjoy exploring ideas!

Narrative/Plot at a Glance

Game	Page	Space Prep	Player Prep	Performance	Group Size	Blocking and Conventions	Characterization	Concentration	Creativity	Ensemble Acting	Group Dynamics	Listening and Silence	Non-Vocal Communication	Observation	Physical Control	Plot Structure	Spontaneity	Equipment
Sherlock Holmes	103	0	10	5-10	4-5	●	●		●	●						●		
The Big Moment	105	0	5	3	3-4	●	●		●	●				●		●	●	
It's a Mystery	107	0	10	5	3	●	●		●	●						●		opt.
Our House	110	0	5	2	4	●	●		●	●						●		
Real Estate Agent	112	0	0	3-5	3	●	●	●						●		●		
Lima Beans	114	0	1	3-4	4-5		●		●	●						●	●	
Glimpses	116	0	5	5	3-4	●	●	●	●	●						●	●	
It's Your Lucky Day!	118	0	0	3-5	3-4	●	●	●	●	●						●	●	
In the Manner of ...	120	0	7	3	4	●	●		●	●						●	●	
It Happened Here	122	0	5	3	4-5	●	●		●	●	●				●	●		
The Birth of the Blobs	126	0	5	2	4	●	●		●	●						●		
Two Thumbs Up!	128	0	10	2	3-4	●	●		●	●						●		
Resolutions	130	0	5	6-10	2	●	●		●	●						●		
A Bird in the Hand	132	0	2	2	3-4	●			●							●		
Rituals	136	0	5	2	4-5	●	●		●	●						●		
In the Lounge	138	0	5	3	3-4	●			●	●						●		
Read All about It	140	0	5	2	5	●	●			●						●		
Magic Shop	144	0	3	3	3-4	●	●		●	●						●		
Super Powers	146	0	0	4-5	4	●	●	●	●	●				●		●	●	
What If?	148	0	1	2-3	3-4	●			●	●						●		
Last Chance Saloon	150	0	2	3-4	3-4	●			●	●						●		
Our Trip to Rio	152	0	5	3-4	4-5	●	●		●	●						●		

Sherlock Holmes

Directions

- Divide the players into groups of four or five.
- Each group receives the title of a "case."
- Groups get ten minutes to decide what the heart of the case might be, why this mystery or crime needs to be solved, and a plan for a scene in which they first became suspicious and decided to call for help from a detective or policeman to solve it.
- The performance will last five to ten minutes.
- After presenting to the entire group and being critiqued, the mystery continues into the next session where the group presents how it was solved.

Example

In "The Case of the Noisy Neighbor," a family in an apartment building is watching TV when they hear noises upstairs. They let us know that new neighbors have just moved in and start to wonder who they are and what they might be like. Suddenly, the noises change and seem unusual. As the family resumes watching the television, the noise becomes more and more suspicious. The group may have made a decision to call in a detective, or they may do another scene the next day as the suspicious noises increase, leading to their call for help. The next scene may focus on the policeman or detective receiving the information and arriving at the scene, only to discover …

Evaluation/Critique

- How was it shown that there was cause for concern/suspicion?
- Did the chosen characters have different reasons to be suspicious? Were these based on their personalities?
- Was tension built? How?
- How did the characters get the detective involved?
- Was the detective involvement satisfactory?
- Was the case "solved" in a satisfying manner?

Challenges and Refinements

- Add a dimension by focusing on specific clues based on situations or objects. (See "Clue Sets" on page 108.)
- Develop this case into an extended mystery of about fifteen to twenty minutes.
- Develop several scenes with cliffhangers at the end of each.
- Develop the detective's personality so that it is quirky, like Sherlock Holmes or Colombo.

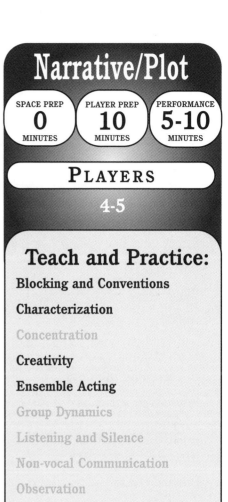

Narrative/Plot

SPACE PREP	PLAYER PREP	PERFORMANCE
0	10	5-10
MINUTES	MINUTES	MINUTES

PLAYERS
4-5

Teach and Practice:

Blocking and Conventions

Characterization

Concentration

Creativity

Ensemble Acting

Group Dynamics

Listening and Silence

Non-vocal Communication

Observation

Physical Control

Plot Structure

Spontaneity

EQUIPMENT
None.

The Case of The ...

Absent-Minded Pharmacist

Amorous Auntie

Angry Acrobat

Battered Barstool

Black Rose

Blood on the Snow

Blue Lake

Bothersome Builders

Boy in the Attic

Broken iPod

Broken Umbrella

Burned Grass

Burnt Christmas Tree

Circus of Wonders

Clown Who Cried

Confused Commuter

Cracked Teapot

Cries from the Box

Cruel Christmas Card

Dangerous DVD

Day That Wasn't

Doctored Cookbook

Dry Well

Evil Earring

Flooded Basement

Frowning Foreigner

Ghost Guest

Haunted Bus

Helpful Hermit

Indolent Iguana

Jaded Gem

Job That Failed

Kindly Assassin

Kinky Clown

Lagoon of Sorrow

Leaking Pen

Locked Attic

Locked Locker

Lonely Lady in Blue

Lost Luggage

Lost Presents

Lost Recipe

Maddening Marauder

Magical Flower Shop

Malevolent Mathematician

Mirror That Lied

Missing Floorboard

Missing Goat

Mysterious Magazine

Naughty Nephew

Nervous Starlet

Noisy Neighbors

Open Coffin

Open Window

Opulent Opals

Paranoid Parrot

Paranoid Pianist

Parrot Frenzy

Pathological Parent

Petrified Flower

Poisoned Cookies

Poisonous Cookbook

Purloined Pencil

Quirky Queen

Road to Nowhere

Runaway Cable Car

Scream in the Kitchen

Scream in the Night

Sensuous Scorpion

Snowman Who Cried

Stolen Dynamite

Stolen Letter

Stolen Lunch Box

Stolen Tennis Shoes

Talking Dog

Terrible Tarantula

Terrible Teenager

Terrified Toddler

Thing in the Sewer

Three Turtles

Trap Door

Troublesome Tourist

Unexpected Author

Unusual Unicorn

Vivacious Vicar

Wrinkled Widow

X-Rayed Xylophone

Yammering Yodeler

Zesty Zebra

The Big Moment

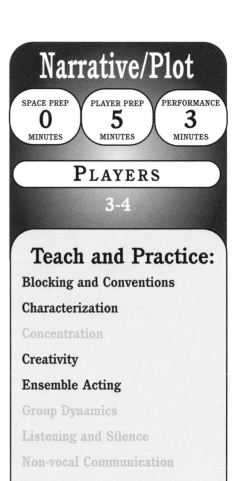

Narrative/Plot

SPACE PREP
0
MINUTES

PLAYER PREP
5
MINUTES

PERFORMANCE
3
MINUTES

PLAYERS

3-4

Directions

- Divide into groups of three or four.
- Each group draws a climax.
- Groups get five minutes to plan a three-minute scene that builds to the climax and ends there.

Examples

- Climax is the phone rings. A group of friends are waiting eagerly in a hospital corridor to hear news about a friend who is in surgery. They are nervously trying to calm down, but the waiting seems interminable. Doctors and nurses pass by, but no one talks to them. They grow more and more nervous until one's cell phone rings. They answer it and crowd around it. The news is bad. End scene.
- Climax is a shot rings out. A family on vacation is trapped in their hotel room because a phone call from reception has told them to stay in their room as a precautionary measure. They are not sure why and are not happy about it. They get more and more annoyed and are just about ready to disobey orders and go out when a shot is heard. End scene.

Side Coaching

- Take enough time in the beginning to set the scene. Introduce your characters and situation.
- Use your middle time to build tension.
- Let all characters build tension in their own ways.
- Work together to heighten tension.

Evaluation/Critique

- Was suspense built? How? If not, what was the result of all the suspense being at the end?
- Was there a clear B-M-E?
- Were the characters developed well?

Challenges and Refinements

- Start the scene from the climax.
- Go beyond the climax and plan some sort of denouement or resolution.
- Plan another climax after this one.

Teach and Practice:

Blocking and Conventions

Characterization

Concentration

Creativity

Ensemble Acting

Group Dynamics

Listening and Silence

Non-vocal Communication

Observation

Physical Control

Plot Structure

Spontaneity

EQUIPMENT
None.

Climaxes

A shot rings out.

A siren goes off.

Everyone collapses, gasping for breath.

Someone backs away.

Someone drops the vase.

Somcone faints.

Someone falls to the ground in a faint.

Someone finds the letter in the book.

Someone jumps out of the closet.

Someone lets go of the balloon.

Someone opens the package and gasps.

Someone picks up the knife.

Someone picks up the phone, and the caller hangs up.

Someone rips up the letter.

Someone shouts, "Brace for impact."

Someone slams on the brakes.

Someone takes a step off the ledge.

Someone throws open the door.

Someone throws the letter down.

Someone tries to get up but cannot.

Someone trips and falls.

The candle sets the curtain on fire.

The corpse in the coffin sits up.

The doctor shakes his head sadly.

The dog bites the child.

The dog gets out.

The doorbell rings.

The lights go on and everyone shouts, "Surprise!"

The lights go out.

The lion escapes from its cage.

The phone rings.

The policeman shouts, "Freeze!"

The robber takes out his gun.

The snake coils to strike.

The window shatters.

There is an explosion.

They all run to the window and scream.

They open the lid of the chest and gasp.

It's a Mystery

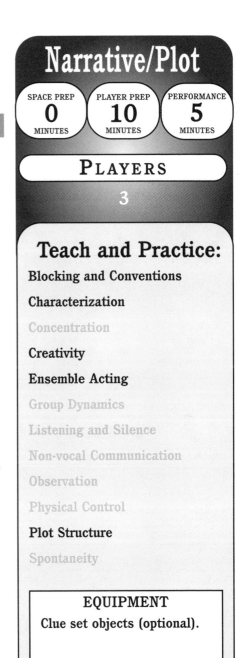

Narrative/Plot

SPACE PREP	PLAYER PREP	PERFORMANCE
0	**10**	**5**
MINUTES	MINUTES	MINUTES

PLAYERS
3

Teach and Practice:
Blocking and Conventions

Characterization

Concentration

Creativity

Ensemble Acting

Group Dynamics

Listening and Silence

Non-vocal Communication

Observation

Physical Control

Plot Structure

Spontaneity

EQUIPMENT
Clue set objects (optional).

Directions

- Divide into groups of three.
- Each group receives a different clue set. This can be actual objects of the director's choosing or the names of the items on cards.
- Using these three clues, the group prepares a mystery to be solved.
- Groups get ten minutes' prep time and then present a five-minute scene to the rest of the groups.

Examples

- Clues are a boom box, key ring, and wine glass. Some friends stop by another friend's apartment (or dorm room). After knocking at the door repeatedly, they enter. A boom box is in the center of the living room blasting some heavy metal. A wine glass is half empty on the coffee table. Where is the friend? At first, they decide he had to leave in a hurry, but then they see the key ring with keys lying on the floor near the bedroom. Slowly, they move to the bedroom. The scene ends.
- Clues are socks, watch, and train ticket. A typical distracted family at breakfast. The man asks his wife to get him socks and she brings him a pair he doesn't recognize. He insists he's never seen them before. Then he goes to put on his watch and finds a totally different one where he keeps his usual watch. When he reaches in his pocket, he removes a ticket stub for a place he has never been. Slowly looking up, he realizes that this is not his family. Cue *Twilight Zone* music …

Evaluation/Critique

- Were the objects all incorporated in the scene?
- Did each one further the plot?
- Was a mystery created?
- Was there suspense?
- Was there a satisfying conclusion?

Challenges and Refinements

- Using these same objects, do a totally different scene with different characters.
- Develop the scene into a mystery with three scenes.
- Make your own clue sets with objects you have lying around, or assign students to bring in their own in brown paper lunch bags.

Clue Sets

paper clip	computer	eraser	fork	jump rope
eyeglasses	sponge	hammer	baseball bat	Monopoly game
tennis shoes	DVD	bicycle	lipstick	belt
apple juice	boom box	wheel	ball	doorknob
magazine	key ring	table	can opener	cassette tape
pen	wine glass	vase	cork	apron
book	note	leaf	Christmas card	coffee mug
telephone	rag	measuring tape	DVD player	bracelet
pen	pillow case	needle	toy car	candlestick
television	remote control	compass	button	wagon
statue	watch	dead flower	cap	toilet paper
safety pin	ring	steering wheel	string	loose diamond
socks	fishing pole	hat	letter opener	toothbrush
watch	chair	pencil	fingernail polish	pillow
train ticket	sheet	cookbook	broken plate	mink coat
paper	box	violin	paper airplane	keys
computer	ring	lighter	tinsel	highlighter
Kleenex	rope	soda can	eyelash curler	business card
pebbles	guidebook	letter	rug	road map
tablecloth	spoon	ashtray	chess piece	empty wallet
bookmark	candle	doorknob	teapot	paintbrush
shoe	photograph	thimble	tea kettle	watercolors
mixing bowl	necklace	puppet	Scotch tape	yardstick
light bulb	stuffed bird	wrench	bow tie	old dress
umbrella	dog leash	mirror	ribbon	lamp
toenail clipper	map	bullet	paper clip	radio
bottle	iPod	candlestick	basket	theatre ticket
mask	light bulb	screw	battery	calendar
watch	scarf	horseshoe	cell phone	postcard
picture frame	playing cards	knife	shoe	bill

marbles
box of cereal
playing card

bow tie
watch
Swiss army knife

matches
thumbtack
colander

guitar
flashlight
pack of cards

handkerchief
corkscrew
comb

rake
toolbox
staples

staple gun
pair of jeans
flashlight

glue stick
computer mouse
needle and thread

scissors
spatula
wine bottle

balloon
digital camera
tray

photo album
iPad
cookie jar

eyelash curler
extension cord
shovel

hair dryer
snow shovel
teapot

teacup
cowboy hat
bottle cap

bowler hat
dollar bill
beach ball

inner tube
wet towel
alarm clock

paintbrush
gloves
toothpaste

credit card
nail
flower pot

handkerchief
old tire
shampoo

sunglasses
electric toothbrush
roller skates

hairbrush
pillow case
aspirin

telescope
pillow
purse

cupcake
placemat
Rubik's cube

broken plate
teddy bear
building block

Legos
lunchbox
backpack

slippers
perfume bottle
tray

paper clip
credit card receipt
hanger

record album
rubber stamp
rubber band

wristwatch
film
dental floss

binoculars
shells
index card

crayons
cat food
coffee grinder

kite
water bottle
bow tie

passport
balloon
cigar

inhaler
piggy bank
credit card receipt

magazine
diary
wrapping paper

Narrative/Plot

SPACE PREP	PLAYER PREP	PERFORMANCE
0	**5**	**2**
MINUTES	MINUTES	MINUTES

PLAYERS

4

Teach and Practice:

Blocking and Conventions

Characterization

Concentration

Creativity

Ensemble Acting

Group Dynamics

Listening and Silence

Non-vocal Communication

Observation

Physical Control

Plot Structure

Spontaneity

EQUIPMENT
None.

Our House

Directions

- Divide into groups of four.
- Each group gets a type of dwelling. This may be either a word or a picture of the dwelling. (Photos of the dwelling or definitions from Wikipedia may be useful.)
- Groups get five minutes to plan a two-minute scene that is suggested by that specific location.

Examples

- Farmhouse. A family has gathered back at the old farmhouse for the funeral of their grandfather, who farmed there all his life. They reminisce about good times spent on the farm.
- Tent. A family tries to set up a tent on a cross-country trip, but disaster ensues as the tent falls down, they are threatened by a bear, etc.

Side Coaching

- Know where everything is in your dwelling. Where are the doors, windows, and important furniture?
- Give us a feeling of size with your blocking.
- Let your senses help us get to know the place. Does it feel cold, large, stable, inviting?
- Use your body as well as your words to respond to the place.

Evaluation/Critique

- Was the atmosphere of the dwelling utilized? How?
- Was there a floor plan with definite elements such as doors, chairs, couches, and stoves? Did these help the story along?
- Did the plot fit the dwelling?
- Were there specific characters who aided the action?
- Was there a clear B-M-E?
- Was the pantomime of the space and objects in it realistic and believable?

Challenges and Refinements

- Put the same characters in a different dwelling.
- Play a totally different scene in the dwelling using different characters.
- Play the same scene in the same dwelling but in a different genre. (See "Genres" on page 121.)
- Play a different scene in the same dwelling but in a different genre.

Dwellings

A-frame

adobe

American craftsman

antebellum plantation home

apartment

barn conversion

barracks

boarding house

boutique hotel

bungalow

bunk house

cabin

camper

castle

cave

cell (jail or prison)

cell (monastic)

chalet

colonial

condominium

cottage

dacha

dorm room

duplex

farmhouse

faux chateau

flophouse

garage

garret

garrison

gatehouse

gazebo

geodesic dome

guest house

hangar

hospital

hostel

hotel

house

houseboat

hut

igloo

inn

lean-to

loft

log cabin

manor house

mansion

mansionette

manufactured home

McMansion

mews

micro-apartment

micro-house

mobile home

motel

mud hut

nuclear bunker/fallout shelter

nursing home

palace

pole house

prefabricated/manufactured

ranch house

rented room

retirement home

roundhouse

row house

sanatorium

shack

shed

sod dug-out

stately home

stilt house

studio apartment

teepee

tent

travel trailer

tree house

underground home

villa

yurt

Narrative/Plot

SPACE PREP	PLAYER PREP	PERFORMANCE
0	0	3-5
MINUTES	MINUTES	MINUTES

PLAYERS

3

Teach and Practice:

Blocking and Conventions

Characterization

Concentration

Creativity

Ensemble Acting

Group Dynamics

Listening and Silence

Non-vocal Communication

Observation

Physical Control

Plot Structure

Spontaneity

EQUIPMENT
None.

Real Estate Agent

Directions

- Divide into groups of three. One player is a real estate agent. The other two players are young prospective buyers.
- The agent shows the property to the buyers. He or she draws an environment card and has to try to convince the buyers to consider the property. The buyers have to adapt to the surroundings.
- The buyers have to decide whether or not they want to purchase the space based on the agent's powers of persuasion. The object is to make the place come alive, to use what it is to "sell" it and create an atmosphere.

Examples

- The agent tries to sell a haunted house. When she realizes that the buyers know the history of this place she downplays the gossip, perhaps even mentioning that there has been an exorcism on it recently. Then, she offers it to them at a low price.
- The agent is selling an old house with hidden passageways. She spins a yarn about how the passageways had been used in the past in very creative ways: for elaborate hide-and-seek games, to hide valuable objects, maybe even for smuggling. Gradually, she realizes that these two people are thieves, and she tries to emphasize the value of the passageways without being too obvious about what she knows.

Side Coaching

- Realtor — Use your body as well as words to paint a picture of this wonderful place. You love it!
- Realtor — Turn every possible objection into an asset.
- Buyers — Listen to the realtor but also "see" for yourself.
- Buyers — Let your questions show the environment.

Evaluation/Critique

- How did the buyers get needed information from the agent?
- Did the agent create a sense of place and atmosphere?
- Were the buyers convinced? Why or why not? How did the agent try to persuade them that this property was the one for them?

apartment over a candy shop

back of a van

baggage room in a train station

barn with farm animals in it

basement apartment with a fold-up bed/couch

battered old place with boarded-up windows and a hole in the floor

bomb shelter

broom-closet-sized opening between two buildings in an upscale part of the city

camper with built-in beds, kitchen, and toilet

cottage on the property of a museum

cozy old home with a huge fireplace and upholstered furniture

Craftsman-style bungalow

curtained-off half of a small room

decrepit old barn in the middle of nowhere

dirt-floored hut

dorm room with two twin beds, a closet, and some shelving

double-wide mobile home

equipment room off a subway station

geodesic dome

haunted house with high ceilings, creaky floorboards, covered furniture, and strange noises

house with all windows and glass walls

houseboat

huge circus tent complete with elephants

hunter's deer blind in a tree

igloo

lean-to on the roof of a department store

lighthouse

log cabin in the woods

low tent

massive tree fort in the middle of a forest

multilevel home with a sunken living room

musty old castle

Native American teepee

nice house next to a squalid one

notorious house where murders have taken place

old '60s style VW van conversion

old house with hidden passageways

opulent palace with marble floors and a sweeping staircase

posh city apartment with a butler

rat-infested wreck

remodeled basement

room in an abandoned prison

spacious, open-plan penthouse with views of the city

subterranean cave

suite at the Four Seasons hotel

tent in a friend's backyard

tenth-floor walkup in an old apartment building

tiny, jail-like cell with a bunk bed, a bookshelf, and a toilet/sink

wine cellar with really low ceilings

SPACE PREP	PLAYER PREP	PERFORMANCE
0	**1**	**3-4**
MINUTES	MINUTES	MINUTES

PLAYERS

4-5

Teach and Practice:

Blocking and Conventions

Characterization

Concentration

Creativity

Ensemble Acting

Group Dynamics

Listening and Silence

Non-vocal Communication

Observation

Physical Control

Plot Structure

Spontaneity

EQUIPMENT
None.

Lima Beans

Directions

- Divide into groups of four or five.
- Each group gets the name of four types of food.
- Groups are given one minute to plan a scene around a meal in a generic dining location (family home, restaurant, school cafeteria) in which the meal consists of only these four foods.

Examples

- Green beans, olive oil, raisins, and a candy bar. Friends meet at a posh new restaurant, all excited about the new chef and his or her daring menu. They are first served raisins in olive oil, and they try to justify to each other how wonderful it is despite being clearly confused. Next course is green beans with nothing else. They become more and more confused. Their dessert is a Hershey bar, which sends them into a rage.
- Basil, cashews, brown rice, and lentils. A family Thanksgiving. Unbeknownst to the rest, the mother has become a vegetarian. She has promised them a low calorie and fascinating meal. The first course is cashews and basil, chopped into a paste, and they aren't given crackers. The family wonders what it is but eats it vaguely. Next comes lentils in brown rice. The mother explains how beans and rice have been used for centuries in healthy balanced meals. When they realize there will be no more food, someone suggests pouring the cashew/basil dish into the lentils and brown rice, and a brilliant new taste is invented.

Side Coaching

- Let the foods suggest the place and situation.
- Physically respond to the different foods as they are presented.

Evaluation/Critique

- Were the foods used creatively?
- Were the characters' reactions suitable to their personalities?
- Did they all have different personalities, or were they similar? How did this affect the plot?

Food

almonds
anchovies
apples
apricots
asparagus
avocados
bananas
barley
basil
beef
beets
bell peppers
black beans
black pepper
blueberries
broccoli
brown rice
Brussels sprouts
buffalo burgers
cabbage
cakes
candy bars
cantaloupe
cashews
cayenne pepper
celery
cheese
chicken
chickpeas
cilantro
cinnamon
cod
cookies
corn
cottage cheese
crab
cucumbers
cumin
dill
donuts
eel
eggplant

eggs
figs
fudge
garlic
grapefruit
green beans
halibut
hazelnuts
ice cream
Jell-O
kidney beans
kiwi
lamb
leeks
lemons
lentils
lettuce
lima beans
limes
lobster
mahi-mahi
meatballs
milk
mushrooms
navy beans
oats
olive oil
olives
onions
oranges
oregano
oysters
papaya
parsley
peaches
peanuts
pears
peas
pecans
pies
pineapple
pinto beans

plums
pork
potatoes
prunes
pudding
pumpkin seeds
raisins
raspberries
redfish
rosemary
saffron
sage
salmon
salt
sardines
scallops
shrimp
soy beans
spinach
squash
strawberries
sunflower seeds
sushi
tarts
thyme
tilapia
tofu
tomatoes
tuna
turkey
turmeric
veal
venison
walnuts
watermelon
wheat
white rice
yams
yogurt
zucchini

Narrative/Plot

SPACE PREP	PLAYER PREP	PERFORMANCE
0	**5**	**5**
MINUTES	MINUTES	MINUTES

PLAYERS

3-4

Teach and Practice:

Blocking and Conventions

Characterization

Concentration

Creativity

Ensemble Acting

Group Dynamics

Listening and Silence

Non-vocal Communication

Observation

Physical Control

Plot Structure

Spontaneity

EQUIPMENT
None.

Glimpses

Directions

- Divide into groups of three or four.
- Each group draws a foreshadowing situation. Foreshadowing is usually defined as a hint of what's to follow. Quite possibly there is a slight undertone of this until it happens.
- Groups get five minutes to prepare a five-minute scene that starts with the foreshadowing situation and builds suspense from there.
- Scenes must have a clear B-M-E with the beginning serving as a foreshadowing situation.
- Scenes may start and end in freezes.

Examples

- Foreshadowing situation is a scream being heard. A family is eating dinner when the scream is heard from outside the front door. Silence as the family tries quietly to decide what to do: wait for another scream, call the police, etc. They dither, getting more and more panicked, until someone outside moans and knocks at the door. Then they slowly move toward the door, open it, and scream in unison.
- Foreshadowing situation is a mirror breaking. A group of girls at a sleepover are putting on makeup when one breaks a mirror. The others tease her about seven years of bad luck, which she brushes off angrily. The teasing resumes until she shuffles off in a huff. A scream is heard.

Evaluation/Critique

- How was it to begin a scene on a high point/conflict?
- If your group chose to begin and end in a freeze, did this work? How?
- Was there clear development that stemmed from the foreshadowing situation?
- Was the B-M-E clear?
- Were there clearly delineated characters?

Challenges and Refinements

- Play the scene but start before the foreshadowing situation.
- Play the scene up to the foreshadowing situation.

Foreshadowing Situations

A black cat crosses your path.

A gypsy tells your fortune.

A siren sounds for hours.

A wave sweeps you out to sea.

It rains for two weeks.

Someone robs you.

While visiting a museum, you break a valuable item.

While working in the garden, you dig up a treasure box.

You are "discovered" at a restaurant.

You are bitten by a dog.

You are caught in a natural disaster.

You are locked in a car.

You are locked in a house.

You are locked out of a car.

You are locked out of a house.

You are mugged.

You are robbed.

You break a mirror.

You break your leg.

You don't recognize someone who claims to be your close friend.

You find a genie in a bottle.

You gain fifty pounds overnight.

You get a call from a long lost friend.

You have to move.

You hear noises in the walls of your new home.

You inherit a family title.

You inherit a million dollars.

You invent something marvelous.

You keep hearing a high-pitched beeping in your living room that no one else hears.

You land a role on a TV show.

You land your dream job.

You lose all of your money in Las Vegas.

You lose your keys.

You lose your memory.

You lose your voice.

You lose your wallet/credit card.

You qualify for the Olympics.

You read your obituary in the paper.

You receive a "Dear John" letter.

You receive a scary crank call.

You see a ghost.

You see a UFO.

You see the person of your dreams across a crowded room.

You start to hear voices.

You suddenly lose your voice.

You wake up with acute hearing.

You win a dream date with your favorite celebrity.

You win an all-expense-paid trip to …

You win the lottery.

Your best friend buys a Porsche.

Your dog runs away.

Your first album goes platinum.

Your local hospital shuts down.

Your three wishes come true.

SPACE PREP	PLAYER PREP	PERFORMANCE
0	0	3-5
MINUTES	MINUTES	MINUTES

PLAYERS

3-4

Teach and Practice:

Blocking and Conventions

Characterization

Concentration

Creativity

Ensemble Acting

Group Dynamics

Listening and Silence

Non-vocal Communication

Observation

Physical Control

Plot Structure

Spontaneity

EQUIPMENT

None.

It's Your Lucky Day!

Directions

- Divide into groups of three or four.
- Each group receives a fortune cookie fortune.
- The scene starts at the end of a meal at a Chinese restaurant when one diner opens his or her "fortune cookie" and reads it aloud.
- The group then improvises the fortune in a "what happened next" scene.

Examples

- Fortune is "It's your lucky day." The group all laughs as the recipient reads the fortune. Suddenly, his cell phone rings. He answers it and listens incredulously to the news. At first it seems tragic — his brother was in an auto accident — but as the conversation continues, it turns out that he is finished at the hospital and just needs a ride home.
- Fortune is "Your life will prosper only when you acknowledge your faults." The other diners tease the recipient until, in tears, she confesses to several unknown misdeeds, one of which was stalking another's boyfriend. The others look on incredulously. At first they're angry, but then they're happy that she has finally admitted it. It turns out that the boyfriend was just arrested for some misdeed, and the friend is grateful to not be associated with him anymore. Everyone congratulates the recipient on her honesty and all is well.

Side Coaching

- Focus on the fortune.
- Stay in your established character as the story unfolds.

Evaluation/Critique

- Did the players have distinct personalities?
- Did each one express an attitude towards the future? Towards the recipient?
- Was the fortune's resolution logical?
- Was there a B-M-E?

Challenges and Refinements

- Develop a post-restaurant scene in which the fortune is acted out.
- Develop a scene in which the opposite of the fortune actually happens.

Fortune Cookies

A focused mind is one of the most powerful forces in the universe.

A great pleasure in life is doing what others say you can't.

A journey of a thousand miles begins with a single step.

Aim high!

Anticipate the difficult by managing the easy.

Bad luck comes to he who wears yellow.

Be patient; the Great Wall wasn't built in a day.

Beware the ides of March.

Don't trust the person sitting next to you!

He who knows does not speak, he who speaks does not know.

Head for the hills!

Health is the greatest possession.

If you do not change direction, you may end up where you are heading.

In every life, some rain must fall.

In order to get the rainbow, you need to endure the rain.

It is better to be a hammer than a nail.

It's never too late for good things to happen.

It's your lucky day!

Jealousy is a useless emotion.

Keep an open mind, but not too open.

Let it be.

Life is short; eat more dessert.

Live your dream!

Look out!

Nirvana is a great disappointment for the ego.

Not sleeping does not mean you're awake.

Remember to always say please and thank you.

Repent! The end of the world is coming.

Resistance is futile.

Respect your ancestors.

See if you can learn anything from children.

Seek your dreams!

Silence is a great source of strength.

Soon you will have many happy days.

Stop searching; happiness is just next to you.

The best is yet to come.

There are big changes ahead for you.

These are the good old days.

Think you can. Think you can't. Either way you'll be right.

Vision is the art of seeing what is invisible to others.

Watch your step!

You are a person with a sense of honor.

You are admired by everyone for your talent and abilities.

You are going to get what you deserve.

You create enthusiasm around you.

You will be judged by what you loved.

You will never amount to anything.

Your dream will come true when you least expect it.

Your heart's desire is at hand.

Your life will prosper only when you acknowledge your faults.

SPACE PREP	PLAYER PREP	PERFORMANCE
0	**7**	**3**
MINUTES	MINUTES	MINUTES

PLAYERS

4

Teach and Practice:

Blocking and Conventions

Characterization

Concentration

Creativity

Ensemble Acting

Group Dynamics

Listening and Silence

Non-vocal Communication

Observation

Physical Control

Plot Structure

Spontaneity

EQUIPMENT
None.

In the Manner of ...

Directions

- Divide into groups of four.
- Each group draws a film/TV genre.
- All the groups perform the same generic scene (a family reunion, a birthday party, or see page 18), but in their own genre.
- Groups have seven minutes to plan a three-minute scene with a clear B-M-E.

Examples

- A birthday party in the style of a biography. Guests arrive for a man's seventieth birthday party and reminisce about highlights of his life.
- A family reunion in the style of a mystery. Family members gather for a reunion but one person, perhaps the hostess, is notably absent. They all search their memories to try to figure out what might have happened to her.

Side Coaching

- Don't play for laughs; if it's funny, the laughs will come.
- Make sure you use the devices of the genre.

Evaluation/Critique

- Was the genre clear?
- Did the genre illustrate the generic scene in a creative and clear way?
- Were the characters differentiated?
- Was there a B-M-E?
- After watching each of the different genres, which one fit the scene best? Why? Which one was the least plausible? Why?

Challenges and Refinements

- Keep the same genre, but change the generic scenes.
- Have all the groups do the same genre and same generic scene. How much variety can you still have?

Genres

action/adventure

biography

buddy/bromance

children's show

cooking show

courtroom drama

crime/detective

docudrama

documentary

dramality (drama/reality)

fairy tale

family drama

fantasy

forensic drama

game show

historical

horror

instructional TV

medical drama

mockumentary

music television

mystery

nature program

news show

political

public affairs

reality TV

romance

satire

science fiction

situation comedy (sitcom)

soap opera/daytime TV

suspense

tabloid television

thriller

variety

Western

SPACE PREP	PLAYER PREP	PERFORMANCE
0	5	3
MINUTES	MINUTES	MINUTES

PLAYERS

4-5

Teach and Practice:

Blocking and Conventions

Characterization

Concentration

Creativity

Ensemble Acting

Group Dynamics

Listening and Silence

Non-vocal Communication

Observation

Physical Control

Plot Structure

Spontaneity

EQUIPMENT
None.

It Happened Here

Directions

- Divide into groups of four or five.
- Each group draws a historical event.
- The group has five minutes to plan a three-minute scene starting and ending with freezes that illustrates a highlight (real or imaginary) of the event. It's OK if the players do not know much about the event.

Examples

- The event is 9/11. Scene starts with a freeze of people grouped around a television watching the event in horror. It unfreezes and they are shown to be a family who has relatives who work in the buildings. They run to the phone but cannot get through. A few minutes later, the phone rings. The scene ends with a look of great relief.
- The event is the moon walk. The scene starts as astronauts are walking on the moon. They unfreeze in slow motion and continue their walk until the flag is planted. The scene freezes until they all group reverently around the flag.

Side Coaching

- You're individuals in the story.
- This isn't a history lesson but a time in history for your character.
- How your character fits in is important.

Evaluation/Critique

- Were the scenes real or imaginary?
- Did they illustrate the event?
- Did they have a B-M-E?

Challenges and Refinements

- Play an imaginary scene with a conflict that takes place during this event.
- Incorporate historical events or current events that the players may be studying in other classes. The players may each be instructed to write one down on an index card and bring it to class.

Historical Events

528 BC — Siddhartha Gautama (563-483 BC) was enlightened under the Bodhi Tree and became the Buddha "Enlightened One." He would spend the rest of his life teaching meditation and mindfulness as a way to enlightenment.

323 BC — Alexander the Great (356-323 BC) built an empire from Greece to India before dying of natural causes at age 33.

221 BC — Shih Huang Ti (259-210 BC), known as the "First Emperor," unified China for the first time. During his Chin Dynasty (221-210 BC), he initiated a centralized government, conducted a census, and standardized the country's currency, written language, laws, and weights and measures. He also began constructing the Great Wall of China.

March 15, 44 BC — Julius Caesar (102-44 BC) was assassinated by disgruntled colleagues after establishing the Roman Empire.

31 BC — Octavian (63 BC-14 AD), Caesar's nephew, defeated Mark Antony (83-30 BC) and Queen Cleopatra (69-30 BC) at the Battle of Actium. Octavian declared himself Emperor Caesar Augustus in 30 BC, marking the birth of Imperial Rome.

December 25, 4 BC — Jesus Christ (4 BC-29 AD) was born in Bethlehem, Roman Palestine, and taught the importance of simplicity, tolerance, meekness, and peace. He was crucified in 29 AD but rose from the dead three days later (Easter).

325 AD — Emperor Constantine (280-337 AD) embraced Christianity and initiated the Council of Nicaea where the differences between Eastern and Western factions of the Christian Church were resolved. The Council drafted the Nicene Creed, the basic Christian beliefs that became the dominant religion in Europe.

476 AD — Last Roman Emperor, Romulus Augustulus (?-476 AD) taken prisoner at Ravenna in 476 AD by German King Odovacar, ending 505 years of the Roman Empire.

July 16, 622 AD — Muhammad (570-632) while meditating near Mecca in 610 AD, had visions from Allah to write the Koran. He escaped from his enemies in Mecca on July 16, 622 and went to Medina. Muhammad's journey (hegira) on this date would mark the birth of Islam.

December 25, 800 AD — Charlemagne (742-814) unified most of Europe under his rule. While attending Mass in Rome, he was unexpectedly crowned "Emperor of the Romans" by Pope Leo III.

October 14, 1066 AD — William of Normandy (1027-1087) crossed the English Channel from France and defeated British King Harold II (1027-1066) at the Battle of Hastings. On Christmas Day, William was crowned King of England and became known as William the Conqueror.

June 15, 1215 AD — At Runnymede, King John of England (1167-1216) signed the Magna Carta, a 63-part document of human rights that became the foundation of the English legal system.

July 19, 1295 AD — Marco Polo (1254-1324) returns from China after a 20-year stay, seeing more of Asia than any other European of his day. His book, *The Travels of Marco Polo*, is one of the most influential travel books in history, inspiring others to find a shorter route to China.

1456 AD — Johann Gutenberg (1400-1468) published the first mass-produced edition of the Bible in Mainz, Germany.

Historical Events

October 12, 1492 — Christopher Columbus (1451-1506) set sail on September 6, 1492 from Castille, Spain with three ships. His expedition landed at San Salvador in the West Indies on October 12, 1492 as he discovers a "New World."

October 31, 1517 — Martin Luther (1483-1546) nailed to the door of Wittenberg Cathedral "95 Theses Against the Sale of Indulgences" detailing the abuses of the Roman Church. This act marked the beginning of the Protestant Reformation in Germany.

August 14, 1708 — Isaac Newton (1643-1727) published the *Principia* where he developed the three laws of motion, demonstrated the structure of the universe and the movement of the planets, and calculated the mass of the heavenly bodies.

July 4, 1776 — The 13 colonies in America met in Philadelphia to sign their Declaration of Independence, declaring themselves free of British rule and taxation.

July 14, 1789 — The French middle class stormed the Bastille, capturing the royal fortress in Paris and starting the French Revolution.

May 18, 1804 — Napoleon Bonaparte (1769-1821) lifted the crown from the Pope's hands and crowned himself Emperor at Notre Dame Cathedral in Paris. He would defeat the Russian and Austrian armies at Austerlitz in December 1805, the Prussians at Jena in 1806, and the Austrians at Friedland in 1807.

June 19, 1815 — Napoleon defeated at Waterloo by Duke of Wellington and was exiled to St. Helena where he died on May 8, 1821.

February 23, 1848 — A revolution in Paris brought the expulsion of King Louis-Philippe and established a Second Republic in France under Louis Napoleon (1808-1873). In this year of revolutions, Prince Metternich fled Vienna to England. Pope Pius IX fled from Rome.

July 8, 1853 — US Navy Commodore Matthew Perry (1794-1858) sailed into Edo Bay, and demanded Japan open its harbors to American trade. The Treaty of Kanagawa was signed on March 31, 1854 to bring Japan's closed feudal monarchy into the world community.

November 24, 1859 — Charles Darwin (1809-1882) published *The Origin of Species,* stating that species evolved because nature selected those animals and plants best suited to specific environments.

April 12, 1861 — The Confederacy attacked a US Army post at Fort Sumter, starting the American Civil War. The four-year war resulted in the death of 364,511 Union troops and 133,821 Confederates.

April 15, 1865 — President Abraham Lincoln (1809-1865) was assassinated at Ford's Theater, Washington DC, by John Wilkes Booth only six days after the end of the Civil War when General Lee surrendered to Grant at the Appomattox Courthouse in Virginia.

January 18, 1871 — Otto von Bismarck (1815-1898) became the Chancellor of the German Empire after defeating the French in the Franco-Prussian War.

March 6, 1876 — "Come here, Watson, I want you." were the first words transmitted through a receiver connected to a transmitter that Alexander Graham Bell (1847-1922) had designed as the telephone.

December 17, 1903 — Wilbur Wright (1867-1912) and Orville Wright (1871-1948) made the first heavier-than-air flight at Kitty Hawk, North Carolina, as their biplane Wright Flyer remained in the air for 12 seconds covering 120 feet.

June 23, 1914 — Archduke Franz Ferdinand (1863-1914) was assassinated in Sarajevo by Bosnian Serbs initiating World War I.

Historical Events

November 7, 1917 — Kerensky's Constitutional Democracy that was set up after the abdication of Czar Nicholas on March 2, 1917 was toppled in a bloody coup on November 7, 1917 by the Bolsheviks under Nikolai Lenin (1870-1924).

December 30, 1922 — Lenin formed the Union of Soviet Socialist Republics, and his Communist Party ruled the country.

October 29, 1929 — New York Stock Market crashed on Black Tuesday where stocks tumbled across the board. It was the most disastrous trading day in the stock market's history. Billions of dollars in open market values were wiped out.

September 1, 1939 — Germany invaded Poland, overrunning it in four weeks. Britain and France declared war on Germany two days later.

December 7, 1941 — Japan attacked Pearl Harbor by surprise. United States entered World War II.

June 6, 1944 — General Dwight David Eisenhower (1890-1969) led the Allied Invasion of Normandy on D-Day. 2.9 million Allied troops, 15,000 planes, and 5,000 ships were mobilized in crossing the English Channel to land on the beaches of Normandy. Paris was liberated from German rule on August 25 and Brussels on September 2.

September 3, 1945 — After the U.S. dropped the atomic bomb on Hiroshima (August 6) and Nagasaki (August 9), Japan officially surrendered on August 15 and formally on September 3 when the signing took place aboard the U.S. battleship USS Missouri in Tokyo Bay.

October 1, 1949 — Chinese Communist Chairman Mao Tse-Tung (1893-1976) declared his country the People's Republic of China after defeating Chiang Kai-Shek's Kuomintang forces who fled to Taiwan.

April 12, 1961 — Soviet Union's Yuri A. Gagarin (1934-1968) became the first man to complete an orbit of Earth.

February 20, 1962 — The first American to orbit the Earth was John Glenn.

July 20, 1969 — Neil Armstrong became the first human to set foot on the moon.

November 1, 1989 — German people attacked the Berlin Wall, chipping it with hammers and bashing it with rocks until the wall came tumbling down. On October 3, 1990, the German Democratic Republic ceased to exist, and the first unified German elections in 58 years were held in December 1990.

November 1, 1989 — Tim Berners-Lee invented the World Wide Web while working at CERN, the European Particle Physics Laboratory in Geneva, Switzerland. He wrote the first WWW client (a browser-editor running under NeXTStep) and the first WWW server along with most of the communications software, defining URLs, HTTP, and HTML.

December 25, 1991 — The hammer and sickle red flag that symbolized 75 years of Soviet communism was lowered for the last time and replaced by 15 flags of 15 newly-independent republics. On January 1, 1992, the Soviet Union and the Soviet Communist Party officially ceased to exist.

SPACE PREP	PLAYER PREP	PERFORMANCE
0	5	2
MINUTES	MINUTES	MINUTES

PLAYERS

4

Teach and Practice:

Blocking and Conventions

Characterization

Concentration

Creativity

Ensemble Acting

Group Dynamics

Listening and Silence

Non-vocal Communication

Observation

Physical Control

Plot Structure

Spontaneity

EQUIPMENT

None.

The Birth of the Blobs

Directions

- Divide into groups of four.
- Each group receives the name of an imaginary band.
- In five minutes, the group plans a two-minute scene with a B-M-E that shows how the band chose their name.

Examples

- The band name is "The Blobs." A group of preteens rehearse a song that a friend of theirs tells them sounds simply terrible. She tries to explain how bad and unfocused it sounds. The group gets more and more annoyed until one of them says, "Are you saying we're just a band of stupid blobs?" and the light bulbs flash on.
- The band name is "Butterfly Effect." A band is rehearsing and keeps getting distracted by a butterfly flying around the room. As they get more and more annoyed, they keep adding interesting new riffs to their song until one of them realizes that they sound really good "because of that annoying butterfly!"

Side Coaching

- When you plan your scene, know what kind of band you are.
- Feel free to play against the name as well as choosing a name that "fits."

Evaluation/Critique

- Did the story tell the origin of the name?
- Was there a clear B-M-E?
- Were there defined characters, or were they generic?
- What kind of music would this band play?

Challenges and Refinements

- Play another scene with a different explanation for the title.
- Play/sing a song from that band.
- Make a list of types of bands, such as punk, rock, folk country, etc. (See "Song Styles" on page 47 for examples.)

Imaginary Bands

666

1666

(Jack the) Rippers

Alone

Alone Together

Anarchy

Appetite

Aroma

Awesomeness

Band of Brothers

Beyond Bad

Black Diamonds

Bling

Blue Light Specials

Blue Plate Special

Bumblebees

Butterfly Effect

Camelot

Cap in Hand

Chain of Fools

Chaos

Chopped Liver

City Lights

Climate Change

Closer

Closet

Complicity

Conspiracy

Cruel Shoes

Daisy Chain

Dancing Dreamers

Davy Jones' Locker

Dawn

Dawn to Dusk

Daydreamers

Dearly Beloved

Dearly Departed

Deus ex Machina

Diamond Dreams

Dog Days

Dusk

Dusk to Dawn

Evolution

Fascinating Rhythm

Machine

Fascinators

Feedback

Floodgates

Flower Bomb

Flying Kites

Forget-Me-Nots

Forgettables

Frankly Speaking

Gift Rapped

Girl Power

Global Warming

Gnarly Waves

Go Figure!

Greensleeves

Horseplay

Iced Cream

Iguana Band

In the Loop

Incendiary Device

Inch Worms

Incubus

Innocence Lost

Intelligence Lost

Jailbait

Komodo Dragons

Ladybugs

Lady Killers

Laryngitis

Lessons

Lights Out

Lizards

London's Eye

Lonely Hearts

Loose Lips

Loss Leaders

Lounge Lizards

Lucy Fur

Merry Widows

Motion Masters

Nervous

Nevermore

No Regrets

Outside the Realm

Overwhelmed

Ozamandeons

Poe's Persuasion

Powder Puffs

Questionable

Rapid Returns

Rattlers

Reggie's Dream

Regrets Only

Revolution

RSVP

Satan's Sinners

Satan's Sister

Sayonara

Scarlet Letter

Seven Neuroses

Singing Sisters

Sisters of Gloom

Sleeping Dogs

Sleeping Gators

Slumdogs

Small Change

Soloists

Sore Loser

Speak Easy

Succubus

Sunken Sister

Sunrise

Sunset

Swing

Technophobia

The Abrasions

The Bullies

The Foreclosures

The Gators

The Geckos

The Go-Bots

The Great Gatsbys

The Leeches

The Lone Rangers

The Long Good-byes

The Mumps

The Pantheon

The Plague

The Pox

The Rat Catchers

The Ravens

The Regrets

The Riots

The Seasons

The Specials

The Translations

Tidal Wave

Tightrope

Titanic

Top Dogs

Tornadoes

Trauma

Travelers

Treasure Seekers

Tsunami

Whipped Cream

Wildcats

Windmills

Windy Days

Wrapping

Narrative/Plot

SPACE PREP	PLAYER PREP	PERFORMANCE
0	**10**	**2**
MINUTES	MINUTES	MINUTES

PLAYERS

3-4

Teach and Practice:

Blocking and Conventions

Characterization

Concentration

Creativity

Ensemble Acting

Group Dynamics

Listening and Silence

Non-vocal Communication

Observation

Physical Control

Plot Structure

Spontaneity

EQUIPMENT
None.

Two Thumbs Up!

Directions
- Divide into groups of three or four.
- Each group draws an imaginary film title and a genre. (For "Genres," see page 121.)
- Groups get ten minutes to prepare a two-minute trailer for this film focusing on the who, what, when, and where of the film.

Examples
- The film is called *Please Return.* Genre: romance. A family takes a vacation to a beach in South America. While there, the teenage daughter meets and falls in love with a handsome beach bum. It is agony to leave him. The girl dreams of him for years, and one day, she returns to the same beach.
- The film is called *Fear Unchained.* Genre: horror. A couple goes to an old hotel in some rural area when they are caught in a storm. A strange bellhop shows them to their room. Later, when they feel strange vibes, they make sure that the chain is in place on the door. In the middle of the night, they hear the chain rattling. When they wake up in the morning, the chain is undone.

Side Coaching
- Use trailer techniques. Show enticing scenes that don't reveal the ending of the film.
- Mix it up with loud and quiet scenes.
- Don't hesitate to repeat a catch phrase.

Evaluation/Critique
- Did the title fit the plot?
- Did the trailer focus on highlights?
- Would you want to see this film based on the trailer?

Challenges and Refinements
- Perform the same basic plot but in a different genre.
- Discuss techniques used in a film trailer to appeal to future audiences. What in a trailer makes you want to go see a movie?

Imaginary Films

A Day to Die For

Across the Stars

Apocalypse Riders

Around the Bend

Ballet Boys

Bus Stop

Daydreamer

Day Tripper

Divorce, American Style

Downsized

Downsizing

Downtown

Far, Far Away

Fashionista

Horsing Around

It's Alive!

Keeping Up with the Joneses

Lazy Days

Learned Lessons

Let's Go to _____ (Name of a Place)

Letter of the Law

Little Sisters

Loose Lips

Losing It

Lost in L.A.

Monroeville

Monsters

More Than Enough

My Big, Fat Fashion Disaster

My Uncle's Castle

Ports of Call

Reunited

Stargazers

Summer Dreaming

Tales of Terror

That Is the End

The Buck Stops Here

Things to Come

Too Much

Towards the Light

Treasurers of the Earth

Uptown

White Men Can't Dance

Who Wants to Marry Me?

Who's to Blame?

Why Not?

Zombie Farm

SPACE PREP	PLAYER PREP	PERFORMANCE
0	5	6-10
MINUTES	MINUTES	MINUTES

PLAYERS

2

Teach and Practice:

Blocking and Conventions

Characterization

Concentration

Creativity

Ensemble Acting

Group Dynamics

Listening and Silence

Non-vocal Communication

Observation

Physical Control

Plot Structure

Spontaneity

EQUIPMENT

None.

Resolutions

Directions

- Divide into pairs.
- In five minutes, devise two scenes — one that shows the problem and another that shows how things have changed since successfully achieving the goal.
- The length of the scenes should be three to five minutes each.

Examples

- Resolution to lose weight. In scene one, a teenager who is very stressed about dating gorges herself on potato chips, and her friend tries to help her by distracting her. But the more the gorger gets stressed and continues eating, the more hopeless she feels. In scene two, the teen has lost twenty pounds. She and her friend are shopping for clothes and she talks about her new life changes. Three different boys have asked her to the prom.
- Resolution to read more. In scene one, a wife is reading the newspaper and getting more and more upset about a political situation. Her husband is ho-hum about it, obviously not knowing or caring about the situation. The wife becomes enraged. In scene two, both are reading, she online and he a book about politics. They start a knowledgeable conversation on some topic and happily decide to go to a public talk on the subject that evening.

Side Coaching

- Go ahead and be dramatic about the situation. That way, the resolution can also be dramatic.

Evaluation/Critique

- Was the problem presented clearly?
- Was the solution logical and satisfying?
- Did the players have distinct characters that fit the logic of the scenes?

Challenges and Refinements

- Using the same resolution, switch characters.
- Using the same resolution, create two totally new plots with new characters.

New Year's Resolutions

act with more confidence

apologize to anyone I've offended

balance work and personal life

be more assertive

be more grateful for what I have

be more open

be nicer to people

change my attitude

change my hair color

clean up the house/garage

drive to work by a new route

exercise more

find a new doctor

get a dog

get a driver's license

get a new job

get a new look

get in touch with old friends

get organized

get out more

go on a diet

go to more concerts

go to more plays

go to the dentist

grow my nails/stop biting my nails

keep up with developments in my field

keep up with the news

learn a new language

learn a new sport

learn to cook

learn to program the DVD player

learn to read a map

learn to read music

lose weight

notice things more

organize my receipts

paint the bedroom

practice my musical instrument

purge my wardrobe

quit smoking/drinking

read more classics (Austen, Dickens)

read more

redecorate

see a therapist

see friends more often

smile more

speak up

spend less time on the computer

spend more time with family

start a new career

stop making stupid remarks

stop talking too much

take singing lessons

travel more

try new recipes

visit museums

watch less news

watch more news

write thank-you notes

Narrative/Plot

SPACE PREP	PLAYER PREP	PERFORMANCE
0	2	2
MINUTES	MINUTES	MINUTES

PLAYERS

3-4

Teach and Practice:

Blocking and Conventions

Characterization

Concentration

Creativity

Ensemble Acting

Group Dynamics

Listening and Silence

Non-vocal Communication

Observation

Physical Control

Plot Structure

Spontaneity

EQUIPMENT
None.

A Bird in the Hand

Directions

- Divide into groups of three or four.
- Each group draws or receives a common saying.
- Groups have two minutes to plan a two-minute scene that illustrates the saying. Keep in mind that the sayings have a universal appeal. They don't have to be used literally in the scenes.

Examples

- Common saying is "A bad workman blames his tools." A family calls for a plumber and gets an apprentice who comes in and causes more trouble. In the process, the apprentice keeps saying that things would have gone better if he had better tools. The family keeps getting him new ones but the problems persist.
- Common saying is "A burnt child dreads the fire." A mother and father keep warning their son not to touch the burners on the stove. Unfortunately, the child does just that and gets badly burned. In the next scene, the mother starts cooking and the little boy runs out of the kitchen.

Side Coaching

- Focus on showing what the scene is.
- Act out the story, don't just talk about it.
- Some of these are serious lessons, but let the saying motivate any humor in the scene.

Evaluation/Critique

- Does the scene illustrate the common saying?
- Was it difficult to illustrate the common saying with a B-M-E scene? How did the group achieve this?
- Was there a clearly defined place where the action occurred?
- Were there distinct characters?
- Were freezes used? If so, were they effective?

Common Sayings

A bad workman blames his tools.

A bird in the hand is worth two in the bush.

A burnt child dreads the fire.

A candle loses nothing by lighting another candle.

A dog is a man's best friend.

A fool and his money are soon parted.

A friend in need is a friend indeed.

A journey of a thousand miles begins with a single step.

A leopard cannot change its spots.

A man is known by the company he keeps.

A penny saved is a penny earned.

A picture is worth a thousand words.

A rising tide lifts all boats.

A rolling stone gathers no moss.

A verbal contract isn't worth the paper it's written on.

A watched pot never boils.

A woman's work is never done.

A word spoken is past recalling.

A word to the wise is enough.

All good things must come to an end.

All publicity is good publicity.

All roads lead to Rome.

All that glitters is not gold.

All's fair in love and war.

An apple a day keeps the doctor away.

An army marches on its stomach.

An ounce of prevention is worth a pound of cure.

April showers bring forth May flowers.

Ask me no questions, and I'll tell you no lies.

Bad news travels fast.

Beauty is only skin deep.

Before criticizing a man, walk a mile in his shoes.

Beggars can't be choosers.

Behind every great man, there's a great woman.

Beware of Greeks bearing gifts.

Birds of a feather flock together.

Blood is thicker than water.

Bloom where you are planted.

Boys will be boys.

Brevity is the soul of wit.

Cleanliness is next to godliness.

Clothes make the man.

Cold hands, warm heart.

Discretion is the better part of valor.

Do as I say, not as I do.

Do as you would be done by.

Don't burn your bridges behind you.

Don't cut off your nose to spite your face.

Don't look a gift horse in the mouth.

Don't throw the baby out with the bathwater.

Don't wash your dirty linen in public.

Early to bed and early to rise makes a man healthy, wealthy, and wise.

Easy come, easy go.

Every cloud has a silver lining.

Every dog has its day.

Every picture tells a story.

Every stick has two ends.

Everything comes to him who waits.

Failing to plan is planning to fail.

Familiarity breeds contempt.

Fight fire with fire.

Finders keepers, losers weepers.

Fire is a good servant but a bad master.

First things first.

Genius is one percent inspiration and ninety-nine percent perspiration.

Give a man a fish, and you feed him for a day. Teach a man to fish, and you feed him for a lifetime.

Common Sayings

Give credit where credit is due.

Give and you shall receive.

God helps those who help themselves.

Great talkers are little doers.

Half a loaf is better than none.

Handsome is as handsome does.

He who hesitates is lost.

He who laughs last, laughs longest.

He who lives by the sword shall die by the sword.

Home is where the heart is.

Honesty is the best policy.

Idle hands are the devil's playthings.

If anything can go wrong, it will.

If it looks like a duck, swims like a duck, and quacks like a duck, then it probably is a duck.

If it's too good to be true, then it probably is.

If life gives you lemons, make lemonade.

If you lie down with dogs, you will get up with fleas.

If you pay peanuts, you get monkeys.

Imitation is the sincerest form of flattery.

In for a penny, in for a pound.

In one ear and out the other.

In order to get where you want to go, you first have to leave where you are.

It ain't over 'til the fat lady sings.

It is the exception which proves the rule.

It takes all sorts to make a world.

It takes one to know one.

It's an ill wind that blows no good.

It's better to be silent and thought a fool than to speak up and remove all doubt.

It's easier to ask forgiveness than permission.

It's easy to be wise after the event.

It's the early bird that gets the worm.

It's the squeaky wheel that gets the grease.

Keep your chin up.

Keep your friends close but your enemies closer.

Kindness, like a boomerang, always returns.

Knaves and fools divide the world.

Knowledge is power.

Laugh, and the world laughs with you. Weep, and you weep alone.

Let bygones be bygones.

Let not the sun go down on your wrath.

Let sleeping dogs lie.

Let the buyer beware.

Life is ten percent what happens to you and ninety percent how you respond to it.

Life is what happens to you while you're busy making other plans.

Life is what you make of it. Always has been, always will be.

Little things please little minds.

Live and let live.

Love is blind.

Love makes the world go 'round.

Make hay while the sun shines.

Make love, not war.

Marry in haste, repent at leisure.

Measure twice, cut once.

Might is right.

Mighty oaks from little acorns grow.

Mind your own business.

Moderation in all things.

Money isn't everything.

Nature abhors a vacuum.

Nature never did betray the heart that loved her.

Nature, time, and patience are three great physicians.

Never judge a book by its cover.

Common Sayings

Never say never.

No man is an island.

No news is good news.

No one can make you feel inferior without your consent.

Old habits die hard.

One good turn deserves another.

One man's junk is another man's treasure.

One rotten apple will spoil the whole barrel.

Opportunity knocks only once.

Paddle your own canoe.

Patience is a virtue.

Possession is nine points of the law.

Procrastination is the thief of time.

Proverbs run in pairs.

Put your money where your mouth is.

Repetition is the mother of memory.

Rules were meant to be broken.

See no evil, hear no evil, speak no evil.

Share and share alike.

Speak softly and carry a big stick.

Sticks and stones may break my bones, but words will never hurt me.

Still waters run deep.

Success has many fathers, while failure is an orphan.

Success is a journey, not a destination.

Talk is cheap.

The apple never falls far from the tree.

The bottom line is the bottom line.

The ends justify the means.

The laborer is worthy of his hire.

The price of liberty is eternal vigilance.

The proof of the pudding is in the eating.

The teacher has not taught until the student has learned.

The whole dignity of man lies in the power of thought.

The world is your oyster.

There is a thin line between love and hate.

There's many a good tune played on an old fiddle.

There's no honor among thieves.

Time and tide wait for no one.

Time flies when you're having fun.

To err is human; to forgive, divine.

Truth is stranger than fiction.

Truth will win out.

Two is company, but three's a crowd.

Use it up, wear it out, make do with, or do without.

Variety is the spice of life.

Walk the walk, and talk the talk.

Walls have ears.

Well begun is half done.

What can't be cured must be endured.

When in Rome, do as the Romans do.

When the going gets tough, the tough get going.

Women and children first.

Wonders will never cease.

You are what you eat.

You can't have your cake and eat it too.

You can't make an omelet without breaking eggs.

You can't teach an old dog new tricks.

You can't win them all.

You catch more flies with honey than with vinegar.

You snooze, you lose.

SPACE PREP	PLAYER PREP	PERFORMANCE
0 MINUTES	**5** MINUTES	**2** MINUTES

PLAYERS

4-5

Teach and Practice:

Blocking and Conventions

Characterization

Concentration

Creativity

Ensemble Acting

Group Dynamics

Listening and Silence

Non-vocal Communication

Observation

Physical Control

Plot Structure

Spontaneity

EQUIPMENT
None.

Rituals

Directions

- Divide into groups of four or five.
- Each group draws a reason to celebrate.
- Groups have five minutes to plan a ritual to celebrate this occasion. Rituals should be two minutes long.
- Be prepared to discuss the idea of ritual. Examples are opening presents on Christmas or Christmas Eve, family gathering for certain meals like Thanksgiving, making pumpkin pie, etc.

Examples

- Celebrating because the sun comes up. Celebrants are meeting at Stonehenge early on the morning of the summer solstice. They gather around the stones, and as the sun rises, they take hands and circle the stones chanting, "Sun! Sun! Sun!"
- Celebrating because you got a raise. Husband or wife comes home with a check for a $10,000 raise. Family gathers in a circle and tells one way the extra money could improve their lives.

Side Coaching

- Don't be afraid to respond to the ritual differently from the others in your group. This is the same ritual, but you are all individuals.

Evaluation/Critique

- Does this ritual reflect the reason for the celebration?
- Is the ritual interesting to watch?

Challenges and Refinements

- Incorporate the ritual into a longer scene about what comes before the cause to celebrate.
- Plan a scene of what happens directly after the ritual.
- Plan a scene in the far-off future after the ritual.

Reasons to Celebrate

It rained.

It snowed.

Someone smiled at you.

The bad neighbors moved out.

The bus was on time.

The coffee is good.

The day is done.

The grass is green.

The house got painted.

The moon is full.

The seasons changed.

The sun comes up.

There was a beautiful sunset.

You ate a lot and didn't gain weight.

You bought a new pair of shoes.

You find a lovely shell at the beach.

You find something you'd lost.

You got a raise.

You got a tan.

You got engaged.

You have a new friend.

You heard a great song on the radio.

You heard from an old friend.

You learned a new dance step.

You like your job.

You lost weight.

You moved to a new house.

You passed an exam with a high grade.

You passed your driver's test.

You reached 500 friends on Facebook.

You saw a great film.

You saw your favorite flower in a window.

You smelled a lovely scent.

You stopped biting your nails.

You witnessed an act of kindness.

You won an award.

Your baby got his or her first tooth.

Your cat had kittens.

Your child learned to ride a bike.

Your favorite color is in style this year.

SPACE PREP	PLAYER PREP	PERFORMANCE
0	5	3
MINUTES	MINUTES	MINUTES

PLAYERS

3-4

Teach and Practice:

Blocking and Conventions

Characterization

Concentration

Creativity

Ensemble Acting

Group Dynamics

Listening and Silence

Non-vocal Communication

Observation

Physical Control

Plot Structure

Spontaneity

EQUIPMENT
None.

In the Lounge

Directions

- Divide into groups of three or four.
- Each group gets the name of a room in the house.
- Groups have five minutes to plan a three-minute scene with a B-M-E that takes place in the room.

Examples

- Scene is in a bathroom. It has been announced that there would be an earthquake, so the family is uneasily filling the bathtub with water when the quake hits, locking them in the upstairs bathroom.
- Scene is in a butler's pantry. The family servants are busily getting items from the pantry for a big state dinner party when all of the items on the top shelf fall, severely injuring the butler.
- Scene is in a cellar. Children break into an abandoned house on a dare. Someone locks them in the cellar, and they find a dead body there.

Side Coaching

- Really give us a sense of place.
- Feel the space so the audience can, too.

Evaluation/Critique

- Was the room clearly defined by the space, use of objects, etc?
- Did the type of room determine the plot?
- How was suspense developed?
- Was it resolved?
- Did the scene have a satisfying B-M-E?
- Were there clearly defined characters?

Challenges and Refinements

- Play a comedy in this room.
- Put the same characters in a different room.
- Choose two rooms and develop a scene that takes place using both rooms.

Rooms in a House

alcove
assembly room
atrium
attic
balcony
ballroom
basement
bathroom
bedroom
billiard room
boiler room
breakfast room
breezeway
butler's pantry
cabinet
carport
cellar
chapel
common room
conservatory
conversation pit
corridor
deck
den
dining room
drawing room
entryway
equipment room
family room
foyer
front room
furnace room
gallery
game room
garage

great chamber
great hall
great room
guest room
gym
hallway
kitchen
kitchenette
laundry room
library
living room
loading dock
loft
lounge
maid's closet
man cave
meditation room
mud room
nook
nursery
office
outhouse
pantry
parlor
play room
porch
powder room
reception room
recreation room
refectory
root cellar
safe room
salon
screening room
scullery

secret passage
servant quarters
shed
shrine room
smoking room
solar
solarium
spice closet
staircase
state room
still room
storage room
storm cellar
study
suite
sunroom
swimming pool
television room
terrace
theatre
undercroft
utility room
vault
veranda
vestibule
walk-in closet
wardrobe
wet bar
wine cellar
workshop

SPACE PREP	PLAYER PREP	PERFORMANCE
0	5	2
MINUTES	MINUTES	MINUTES

PLAYERS

5

Teach and Practice:

Blocking and Conventions

Characterization

Concentration

Creativity

Ensemble Acting

Group Dynamics

Listening and Silence

Non-vocal Communication

Observation

Physical Control

Plot Structure

Spontaneity

EQUIPMENT
None.

Read All about It

Directions

- Divide into groups of five.
- Each group receives two nouns, a verb, and an adjective.
- Groups get five minutes to plan a two-minute scene with a B-M-E that is based around this headline.
- Sometimes the word combinations just do not make sense. The group has permission to change, add, or subtract one word. A list of real headlines is included for examples.

Examples

- "Little kids," "Hogwarts students," "jump," and "angry" become "Little Kids Jumped Angry Hogwarts Students." A gang of Muggle children is out causing trouble when they stumble upon some similarly aged Hogwarts students. They try to jump them but soon find that the wrath of wizards is dangerous.
- "Journalists," "snakes," "killed," and "posh" become "Posh Journalists Killed Snakes." A group of well-dressed journalists are covering a fashion show in Paris when screams are heard from backstage. Sensing a story, they rush back only to find the models besieged by snakes. They shed their posh clothes and jump in, killing the snakes with their computers, stilettos, or whatever.

Side Coaching

- When you're planning, try different combinations of your words until you find the right one.
- Use pieces of paper with one word on each to devise your headline.

Evaluation/Critique

- Did the headline make sense?
- Did it determine the plot?
- Was there a B-M-E?
- Were there clear characters?
- Did the scene have conflict?

Challenges and Refinements

- Turn the scene into a news broadcast complete with interviews and filmed footage. Was it more or less interesting?
- Change a noun, and then redo the scene.

Scrambled Headlines

Nouns
(Choose Two)

Aliens

Apple

Astronaut

Backpack

Barbers

Beach Blanket

Bell

Bigfoot

Bomb

Book

Bouncer

Business Card

Button

Cake

Car

Car Salesmen

Cat

Caterpillars

CD

Cell Phone

Cereal

Chair

Clowns

Coffee Cup

Computer

Computer
   Programmers

Contact Lens

Corrupt Politicians

Dentists

Diamond Ring

Doctors

Dog

Dog Catcher

Doll House

Door-to-Door
   Salesmen

Doorman

DVD

Fisherman

Flower Pot

Football Hooligans

Frying Pan

Game Show Emcee

Gang Members

Garbage Can

Gas Station
   Attendant

Ghosts

Glasses

Gun

Hammer

Hamster

Headphones

High Heels

Hit Men

Hogwarts Students

Horse

Housewives

Insurance Agents

iPad

Janitor

Journalists

Judge

Juvenile Delinquents

Key

Knife

Letter

Lion Tamer

Lipstick

Little Kids

Loch Ness Monster

Lunch Lady

Magazine

Magnet

Mayor

Mice

Microwave Oven

Mother

Muffin

Nail

Needle

Newspaper

Nobel Prize Winners

Nuns

Olympic Athletes

Orchestra Conductor

Paintbrush

Paper Towel

Paper Clips

Pea

Perfume

Pharmacists

Pie

Pigs

Pill

Pizza

Plumbers

Poison

Priests

Prisoners

Psychiatrists

Quilt

Radio

Rats in the Sewer

Refrigerator

Repairmen

Rock Star

Rope

Running Shoes

Sandbox

School Principal

Security Guard

Shampoo

Shoe

Siamese Cats

Snakes

Soap

Soldiers

Sportscasters

Stapler

Statue

Students

Taxi Driver

Teacher

Teddy Bear

Telephone

Tennis Players

Ticket

Tiger

Tooth

Tourists

TV Guide

Umbrellas

Vase

Waiters

Wasp

Water Bottle

Wine Bottle

Wrench

Zombies

Scrambled Headlines

Verbs (Choose One)

Ate

Bit

Broke

Bullied

Carried

Cavorted

Choked

Confused

Conspired

Controlled

Convinced

Cursed

Cut

Cycled

Danced

Destroyed

Discussed

Drank

Drew

Drove

Escaped

Fell

Flew

Fooled

Grinned

Hugged

Hypnotized

Jumped

Kicked

Kidnapped

Killed

Kissed

Laughed

Lied

Located

Looted

Moved Away

Painted

Punched

Punished

Pushed

Ran

Read

Rioted

Ripped Through

Robbed

Scratched

Screamed

Sculpted

Shipped

Skated

Slept

Stabbed

Stared

Stole

Taught

Tripped

Washed

Whispered

Yelled

Adjectives (Choose One)

Angry

Athletic

Attractive

Bewildered

Brave

Cautious

Clumsy

Compassionate

Confused

Cowardly

Cranky

Curvy

Dangerous

Devious

Dirty

Dishonest

Fake/Phony

Fat

Fearful

Flirtatious

Foul-Mouthed

Frightened

Frightening

Frustrated

Giggly

Happy

Harmless

Heroic

Hideous

Homeless

Honest

Hostile

Humorous

Infectious

Insane

Intelligent

Lazy

Lonely

Loud

Messy

Mischievous

Miserly

Murderous

Nervous

Nosy

Paranoid

Perky

Poisonous

Poor

Posh

Rich

Rude

Sad

Shiny

Shrewd

Simple

Sly

Smelly

Stupid

Suspicious

Tattooed

Ugly

Venomous

Real Headlines

Alleged Burglars Return to Apologize

Breakthrough in Canada's Great Maple Syrup Heist

Burglar Hung Wreath, Watched TV

Café Full of Cats Opens in Vienna

Candy Thief Targets Peanut Butter Cups

Car Lands on Roof of Apartment after Wreck

Dog Eats $4,500 Wedding Ring

Family Says Home Invaded by Opossums

Family Wakes to Find Lexus in Pool

Fight with Deer Leaves Man with Black Eyes

Five-Inch Worm Found in Man's Eyeball

Frosty the Snowman Arrested at Parade

Fugitive Who Noted Escape on Facebook Arrested

Giant Rodents Found in Florida Keys

Half Man, Half Bird, All Awesome

High School Puts Itself up for Sale on eBay

Horse Rider Arrested for Fighting

Child Bitten by Rabid Bat after Strange Woman
Tells Her to Hold It

Judge Falls Asleep during Trial — Twice

Man Accidentally Dials 911 during Theft

Man Accused of Blowing up Candy House

Man Arrested in Lightsaber Attack

Man Attacks Roommate with Ukulele

Man Breaks into Home to Watch TV

Man Changes Name to Tyrannosaurus Rex

Man Dies after Live Roach-Eating Contest in Florida

Man Faces Prison over Flaming Marshmallows

Man Fears False Teeth Eaten by Dog after Fight

Man Jailed for Stabbing Woman at Her Request

Man Made 911 Call during Drug Deal, Cops Say

Man Orders TV on Amazon, Gets Assault Rifle

Man Rescued from Own Chimney

Man Sets Fire to Home by Microwaving Socks, Undies

Man Tries to Use $1M Bill at Wal-Mart

Man Trying to Sell Son on Facebook for $20M

Man Waits on Hold for Fifteen Hours

Man Wakes up at Own Funeral

Man Who Lost Hand Charged with Feeding Gator

Mickey Mouse Spurs School Lockdown

New York Inmates Sue Over Dental Floss

Newspaper Must Pay Readers for Exploding Churros

Penguin Stolen from Theme Park

Philanthropist's Death Sparks Unusual Lawsuit

Phone Left in Plane's Restroom Triggers Bomb Scare

Pilot Turns Back after Snake Pops out of Dashboard

Puppy Gets Drunk on Owner's Vodka and Coke

Python Latches onto Woman's Face

School Employee Faked Daughter's Death

Spider Found Living in Woman's Ear

Stick Shift Stops Robber until Victim Offers Ride

Stranger's Seeds Get Grandma in Trouble

Suspect Arrested after Flirting with Cop

Thieves Steal from Suspected Shoplifters

This Cow Head Will Supposedly Exorcise Demons
on a Ship

TSA Confiscates Cupcake; Frosting a Risk

Two Kids, Determined to Reach Santa, Call 911

Woman Blamed Party Noises on Ghost

Woman Buys Two Rats, Soon Has 71

Woman Hit with $1.3 Million-Plus Electric Bill

Woman Puts 'Soul' up for Sale on eBay

Woman Runs Over Husband in Voting Dispute

Woman Says McNugget Looks Like President

Woman Spends Summer as Mermaid

Woman Spots Her Child for Sale on Internet

Woman with ZOMBIE Plates Accused of Attack

Young Historian Spots Museum Error

Zoo Puts Stuffed Animals in Cages to Cut Costs

Narrative/Plot

SPACE PREP	PLAYER PREP	PERFORMANCE
0	3	3
MINUTES	MINUTES	MINUTES

PLAYERS

3-4

Teach and Practice:

Blocking and Conventions

Characterization

Concentration

Creativity

Ensemble Acting

Group Dynamics

Listening and Silence

Non-vocal Communication

Observation

Physical Control

Plot Structure

Spontaneity

EQUIPMENT
None.

Magic Shop

Directions
- Divide into groups of three or four.
- Groups get the name of a real or imaginary type of shop.
- Groups get three minutes to plan a three-minute scene that takes place in the shop.
- The type of shop must determine the plot.

Examples
- Shop is a detective agency. A nervous couple comes to the detective agency only to find a very elderly woman is the detective. They wanted her to find who is terrorizing them at night but get concerned that she is not up to the job. She convinces them that she is.
- Shop is for lost items. A man has left a bottle of shampoo in a taxi and comes to the shop of lost items to look for it. The shop is a maze of weird objects, and the proprietor is a very strange person indeed.

Side Coaching
- Customers — Why are you in the shop? Are you anxious? Skeptical?
- Proprietor — Are you helpful, pushy, indifferent? Will your product sell itself, or do you need to work at it?

Evaluation/Critique
- Did the plot fit the setting?
- Did the setting help with the plot?
- Was the scene developed?
- Was there a B-M-E?
- Was there suspense? Humor?
- Were there specific characters?
- Did the shop have definite objects in it?

Challenges and Refinements
- Play the scene that led to the people going to the shop.
- Play a scene after they have left the shop.
- Play a scene in which a crime takes place in the shop and is solved using the theme of the shop.

Shops

advice
antiques
arguments
art gallery
baby clothes/supplies
bakery
books
butcher
buttons
buy a feeling
calm down
camera
candy
children's books
chocolate
coffee
computer
curses anonymous
detective agency
Disney
dive
dollar store
donuts
dry cleaners
DIY
escape
face lifts
find the right word
fishing tackle
flower
fortune tellers
furniture
greeting card

groceries
hair and beauty supplies
hair salon
hardware
Harry Potter
hire an actor
hire an apprentice
hire an impressionist
jewelry
joke store
kitchenware
knives
laundromat
left-handers supplies
liquor
lonely hearts
lost causes
lost items
love potions
luggage
luggage repair
magic
makeup
masks
mind expansion
new age
nostalgia
office supplies
perfect gifts
perfume
pet
pharmacy
picnic supplies

picture framing
plan your own disappearance
poisons
pun
puppets
questions answered
rejuvenation
religious items
rocks and minerals
sewing
shoe
skateboard supplies
sleep
sock
souvenir
swimwear
tea
teddy bears
theatre tickets
thrift/charity
ties
toys
travel supplies
truth tellers
underwear
used clothing
vitamins
wake up
women's clothes
wordsmith
write your own book
write your own story

SPACE PREP	PLAYER PREP	PERFORMANCE
0	0	4-5
MINUTES	MINUTES	MINUTES

PLAYERS

4

Teach and Practice:

Blocking and Conventions

Characterization

Concentration

Creativity

Ensemble Acting

Group Dynamics

Listening and Silence

Non-vocal Communication

Observation

Physical Control

Plot Structure

Spontaneity

EQUIPMENT
None.

Super Powers

Directions

- Divide players into groups of four.
- Each player gets a super skill or trait.
- With no time for prep and without knowing the other players' powers, the group plays a scene in which they are college suitemates who have just met and are trying to get to know each other.
- The scene lasts four to five minutes.

Example

A has the gift of stopping war. B always tells the truth. C can read past lives. D can find lost objects. The suitemates sit on the couch and chairs and introduce themselves. B starts making astute observations, such as how he can sense that everyone feels nervous. C makes a comment about how A must have been Freud in his past life. A tries to stop any conflict and suggests they make some coffee. He goes to the kitchen to find it. D volunteers to find it, but stops at the couch with his eyes closed.

Side Coaching

- Keep thinking about what your character can do with your super power.
- Work to interact with each other even if you aren't sure what your partners' super powers are.
- Listen to everyone's hints as well as concentrating on making yours obvious.
- Show, don't tell.

Evaluation/Critique

- How were these super powers made to seem somewhat realistic? Or were they?
- Did the powers cause conflict, further the action, and determine what would happen?
- How did the players manage to get along with each other in character?
- Were the characters they portrayed believable with these powers?

Super Skills

always knowing the right thing to say

being incredibly interesting

being the perfect parent

breathing underwater

calming children

casting spells

changing size

climbing anything

creating calm

deflecting anger

erasing memories

fashion sense

finding lost objects/people

flying

giving perfect advice

good taste

healing

helping people lose weight instantly

hypnotizing people into doing what you want

incredible athletic ability

interpreting dreams

invisibility

making everyone happy

making money

making people fall in love with you

making the elderly young again

matchmaking

memorization

mind reading

perfect balance

perfect taste

predicting the future

producing works of art

reading past lives

seeing the future

shape shifting

solving conflicts

solving difficult problems

speaking to the dead

stopping storms

stopping time

stopping wars

stretching

super multitasking

talking to animals

telling the truth

time travel

turning invisible

understanding all languages

walking through walls

Narrative/Plot

SPACE PREP
0
MINUTES

PLAYER PREP
1
MINUTES

PERFORMANCE
2-3
MINUTES

PLAYERS

3-4

Teach and Practice:

Blocking and Conventions

Characterization

Concentration

Creativity

Ensemble Acting

Group Dynamics

Listening and Silence

Non-vocal Communication

Observation

Physical Control

Plot Structure

Spontaneity

EQUIPMENT
None.

What If?

Directions

- Divide players into groups of three or four.
- Give each group the name of a "thing you'd like to see."
- The scene is set in the future when this "thing" has just been invented.
- Create a television commercial for it, showing scenes of it in use.
- Groups get one minute to plan, and scenes should last two to three minutes.

Examples

- Product is "IQ-raising pills." Scene is in a classroom where a child is being bullied for her grades. Scene is frozen. Teacher calls to student and slips her a pill. The next scene shows the child getting all As and the rest of the students looking totally confused as a newscaster announces the product as "Smart Parts."
- Product is "no death." Scene is a hospital. A family is gathering around the bed of an elderly relation who "dies." All mourn. Suddenly, the "corpse" sits up and speaks, then "dies again." A doctor is called who declares him dead. He sits up again. Everyone is confused. Broadcaster enters and tells audience that for only ten million dollars, death has been eradicated, and this person bought a "death insurance policy" to surprise his loved ones.

Side Coaching

- What are the benefits of this product?
- What are the negative sides of your product?
- Will you balance the good and bad or stress one over the other?

Evaluation/Critique

- Did the scene fit the "new thing"?
- How were scene changes handled? Were freezes used?
- Did the players have specific characters? Did these enhance the scene?

Challenges and Refinements

- Prepare before and after scenes with the new "thing."
- Play a scene in which this new "thing" does more harm than good.

Things You'd Like to See

3D phone conversations

a pill for everything that ails you

affordable deep-sea travel

affordable space travel

animal translation

anti-gravity machines

automatic hairstyling

candy grams

elevated sidewalks

flying cars

food-flavored pills

free food

free healthcare

free housing

happiness pills (not anti-depressants)

high-speed trains/planes

holographic teachers

homework machine

honest politicians

immortality

instant weight loss pills

instantly available babysitters

instantly available dog walkers

instantly available food

instantly available massage

invisibility cloak

IQ-raising pills

job-swapping programs

lifelong learning opportunities for all

no death

non-toxic steroids

non-weight-gain food (no-calorie food?)

perfect matchmaking

post-life viewers

push button cleaning

relaxation booths

rent-a-pet

shape shifting opportunities

spirit communication

telepathic communication

temporary face lifts (non-surgical)

time machine

talking animals

transporters

truth tellers

weather control

Narrative/Plot

SPACE PREP	PLAYER PREP	PERFORMANCE
0	2	3-4
MINUTES	MINUTES	MINUTES

PLAYERS

3-4

Teach and Practice:

Blocking and Conventions

Characterization

Concentration

Creativity

Ensemble Acting

Group Dynamics

Listening and Silence

Non-vocal Communication

Observation

Physical Control

Plot Structure

Spontaneity

EQUIPMENT
None.

Last Chance Saloon

Directions

- Divide players into groups of three or four.
- Each group draws the name of an unusually named town.
- Groups have two minutes to prepare a scene that is based on the name of the town.
- The scene lasts three to five minutes.

Examples

- Welcome to the town of Fear Not. Fear Not is a town in the Old West. The scene takes place in a saloon where brave cowboys are planning to defend the town against a gang of robbers who are about to descend on them. Each one brags of his or her prowess in fighting until a lone gunman walks in and they freeze in horror.
- Welcome to the town of Mystic. Mystic is a little town in Montana with the highest number of psychics in the world. The scene takes place at a psychic convention where a group of tourists come to have their fortunes told.

Side Coaching

- When planning, you may choose how your town got its name, what living in it is like, occupations of people in your town, etc.
- Be open to all ideas.

Evaluation/Critique

- Was the town's name useful in establishing a sense of place?
- Did the sense of place determine the plot?
- Was an environment created? How?
- Were there interesting characters?
- Was there a clear B-M-E?

Challenges and Refinements

- Plan a scene in the same town that belies the name of the town. (The people in Coward are all heroes. The people in Oddwill are completely normal, etc.) How would the incongruity affect the type of scene?
- Play a different scene in the same town.
- Move the scene to a different part of town. (Saloon becomes a hospital; convention center becomes a school, etc.)

Unusual Town Names

Aimwell
Alligator
Antler
Arcade
Aromas
Avocado
Bad Ace
Bad Water
Badger
Bald Knob
Bat Cave
Belcher
Big Chimney
Big Sky
Birdsong
Black Jack
Blue Eye
Boneyard
Boring
Bowlegs
Bridal Veil
Buddha
Bumble Bee
Burns Downs
Buttermilk
Buzzard's Roost
Camel Hump
Camel Rock
Carefree
Christmas
Cocked Hat
Cokeville
Cold Water

Concrete
Cookie Town
Cow Creek
Coward
Croaker
Cut and Shoot
Cyclone
Date City
Dead Horse
Dead Woman
Crossing
Ding Dong
Dragon
Due West
Dull
Eclectic
Eden
Elmo
Embarrass
Eureka
Fallen Leaf
Famous
Fear Not
Fickle
Fishhook
Fleatown
Floss
Forks
Fox Den
Frankenstein
Friendly
Gas City
Goober Town

Greasy Corner
Gripe
Hallelujah Junction
Happy Land
Hell
Hells' Kitchen
Hog Jaw
Hoop and Holler
Hungry Horse
Hurricane
Hurt
Idiotville
Imalone
Index
Jackpot
Java
Junky
Kermit
Last Chance
Liberal
Little Hope
Looneyville
Lost City
Manly Hope
Mars
Mashpee
Muck City
Muddy Gap
Mystic
Needmore
Niceville
Nothing
Nuckles

Ocean Roar
Oddville
Orderville
Ordinary
Parade
Paradise
Paradox
Pie
Plain City
Pocket
Pyro
Rainbow
Ransom
Red Head
Red Shirt
Rifle
Ringer
Rising Sun
Robbers
Robin Hood
Sandwich
Santa Claus
Secret Town
Shoofly
Skull Valley
Slaughterville
Sleeper
Sleepy Eye
Sleepy Hollow
Slippery Rock
Snaketown
Snowball
South Border

Spider
Spraytown
Success
Sweet Lips
Three Forks
Tick Bite
Tiger Bay
Tin Cup
Toad Hop
Toad Suck
Tombstone
Trickem
Troll
Truth or
 Consequences
Turkey
Two Guns
Type
Ubet
Uncle Sam
Useful
Veribest
Volcano
War
Weedpatch
Weeping Water
Welcome
What Cheer
Why
Whynot
You Bet
Yum Yum
Zap

Narrative/Plot

<table>
<tr><td>SPACE PREP
0
MINUTES</td><td>PLAYER PREP
5
MINUTES</td><td>PERFORMANCE
3-4
MINUTES</td></tr>
</table>

PLAYERS
4-5

Teach and Practice:

Blocking and Conventions

Characterization

Concentration

Creativity

Ensemble Acting

Group Dynamics

Listening and Silence

Non-vocal Communication

Observation

Physical Control

Plot Structure

Spontaneity

EQUIPMENT
None.

Our Trip to Rio

Directions

- Divide into groups of four or five.
- Give each group the name of a vacation destination.
- Using this destination, each group has to plan and perform a scene with a B-M-E that could only take place in this particular location.
- Groups have five minutes to plan, and the scene should last three to four minutes.

Examples

- Destination is Rio de Janeiro. A group of college students on a winter break decide to visit the Carnaval in Rio. After a long and delayed flight, the fatigued students arrive in Rio and have to go to the parade before they even check in to their hotel. They find a place on the street to watch the floats, but a thief steals one of the students' suitcases and runs off into the parade. The students chase him into the parade.
- Destination is a dog show. A very wealthy but bored old woman enters her prize poodle into a local dog show. When she arrives, her dog is attacked by larger dogs and runs away. The old woman has to shed all her fancy trappings to give chase and finally catches the poodle, now looking disgraceful. She enters him anyway, and he wins in the category of the "most unusual dog."

Evaluation/Critique

- Did the scene have a definite B-M-E?
- Were there distinctive characters?
- Was the destination used creatively and logically?
- Were there specific objects in this place that played a part in the scene?
- Was there conflict? How was it resolved?

Challenges and Refinements

- Using the same setting and characters, perform a completely different plot.
- Have a disaster occur in this setting.
- Have a crime occur and solve it using the setting as an important player in the crime. (A drowning at a beach, food poisoning at a gourmet food tasting, etc.)
- Make laminated cards with photos of various destinations on them. On the back, make lists of events that might happen there and/or physical characteristics of the places.

Vacation Destinations

Africa

ashram

archaeological site

barge tour

beach

bicycle trip

bigfoot convention

carnival

cave

Chelsea Flower Show

Christmas market tour

circus

college visit

convention (Star Trek, etc.)

cottage by a lake

cruise to Alaska

Disney World

Disneyland

dog show

dogsled races

dude ranch

family graves

family reunion

famous castle

famous cathedral

Fashion Week (New York, Paris, Milan)

fat farm (weight loss camp)

fiery food convention

forest

gambling vacation

Hawaiian volcano tour

healing shrine

hiking trip

historical tour

Hollywood

holy lands

horse race

horseback riding on a beach

Las Vegas

Lego Land

London

mountains

national park

new department store

northern lights tour

Oktoberfest

old amusement park

organic farm

Paris' Eiffel Tower

penthouse apartment

photographic safari

photography tour

pilgrimage (Mecca, etc.)

religious retreat

Rome

safari

skiing

summer camp

surfing

Swiss chalet

theatre tour

theme park

Tibetan monastery

tropical island

UFO gathering

world heritage site

The Answers at the Back of the Book

Animals of the Chinese Zodiac

The New Lunar Year, or Chinese New Year, marks the beginning of the Chinese calendar. Each year is named after one of twelve animals. There are as many stories of how the Chinese zodiac years got the names of animals as there are storytellers. This is one of our favorites. It's based on a great race.

The Invitation and a Grand Race

A long, long time ago, the Jade Emperor invited all the animals in the world to visit. Imagine how disappointed he was when only fourteen showed up. To honor the ones who came, he promised to name a year after each one. But how to decide who would have the first year named after him? The Emperor decided to have a race on the following day and asked the very wise Elephant to act as the judge. That is why there is no "Year of the Elephant." The race would take the animals over a long course of varied terrain and end with a swim over the river near the palace. The Emperor gave a magnificent banquet with the favorite food of each animal. After dinner, they retired to sumptuous quarters to rest before the big race the next day.

Cat and the Rat

In those days, the Cat and the Rat were best friends. The Cat always took his own sweet time to wake up, so fearing he might miss the grand race, he asked his friend the Rat to wake him up the next morning. The Rat, however, forgot his promise and left without his best friend the Cat. When the Cat finally woke up, it was already too late. The Cat did not get to the race on time, and hence, there was no year in the Chinese zodiac named after him. That is why, to this day, the Cat will always hunt the Rat.

Some people say the Rat forgot on purpose, but we like to think the Rat was actually too excited about being in the race, and that's why he didn't wake up his friend the Cat.

The Rat and the Ox

When the Rat got to the race, he saw other animals in front of him. They all ran much faster than he, and many were good swimmers, too. In order not to fall behind them, he had a brilliant idea. He knew that the Ox was a steady runner and the mightiest swimmer and being a very straightforward animal, would believe anything. So he pleaded with the Ox to let him ride on its head and tried to convince the Ox that he, being a small animal, will not be able to run faster than him. The Ox agreed. As they neared the shore at the end of the race, the Rat quickly jumped off and sprinted to the finish line. The Rat was the first to arrive, followed by the Ox. The first year in the Chinese zodiac calendar is therefore named after the cunning Rat and the second after the Ox.

The Tiger

Not far behind was the Tiger. Although the Tiger is a fast animal, he had a problem crossing the river. The heavy current kept pushing him downstream. With all his might, he finally managed to get to shore and came third in the race. So the third year of the Chinese Zodiac calendar is named the "Year of the Tiger."

The Rabbit

The Rabbit was next. He was wet and exhausted. He had tried to cross the river by jumping from stone to stone but lost his balance, fell in, and almost drowned. Fortunately, he managed to grab a floating log and drifted on it to shore very close to the finish line. So the fourth year in the Chinese Zodiac calendar is the "Year of the Rabbit."

The Dragon

Although the Dragon can fly, he only came in fifth. Making rain and wind for the people on earth was his job. He heard a plea for rain and detoured to do his job. He also saw the poor Rabbit holding on to the log, struggling to stay afloat. So he puffed and puffed his breath to push the log to shore. The Rabbit never realized that the Dragon saved him. That is why babies born in the "Year of the Rabbit" always enjoy good fortune in the "Year of the Dragon."

The Horse and the Snake

As soon as the Dragon took his seat next to the Rat, Ox, Tiger, and Rabbit, the Horse came charging in. He thought that he would be the sixth animal to arrive, but he was wrong. Unbeknownst to the Horse, the Snake had clung on to his leg, and the moment they were about to reach the finish line, the Snake jumped. At that moment, the Horse, taken by surprise, shied backward and lost to the Snake, who claimed the sixth position.

The Goat, Monkey, and Rooster

Moments later, the Goat, Monkey, and Rooster came in almost together. Just before crossing the river, the Rooster saw the Monkey and the Goat. He thought it would be better if they worked together to cross the river rather than doing it all by themselves. Together, they made a raft. But it wasn't easy with all three of them on a small raft. They had to push and pull and finally managed to cross the river. Running to the finish line, the Goat managed to arrive first, followed by the Monkey and then the Rooster.

The Dog and the Pig

Although the Dog is a good swimmer, he came in at eleventh place. He was a playful animal and splashed around in the water too much, letting the others overtake him. Long after all the eleven animals had arrived, the Pig finally appeared. In fact, the Jade Emperor had given up hope of any more animals arriving when they heard the familiar *oink, oink.* The Pig, who was always hungry, had stopped to eat in the middle of the race. He ate too much, grew sleepy, and dozed off. He was lucky to wake up just in time to come in twelfth.

Aligning Improv Games to the National Standards for Theatre Education

About the National Drama Standards

This list may act as a reference indicating drama skills addressed in the games and can also help with lesson plans, as many state theatre standards reflect the national standards. Please see resources at the American Alliance for Theatre Education's website at www.aate.com.

The following standards are for grades 5-8. Standards for K-4 and 9-12 are also available at www.aate.com. **Theatre standards regularly fulfilled by the games in this book are in normal print and are the only ones on the charts following the description. Additional standards are in italics and complete a drama curriculum.** Justine Jones and Mary Ann Kelley have written two curricula that address all drama standards: *Drama Games and Improvs* and *Staging an Interactive Mystery Play.* Both are available from Meriwether Publishing Ltd. at www.meriwether.com.

Content Standard 1

Script writing by the creation of improvisations and scripted scenes based on personal experience, heritage, imagination, literature, and history.

Achievement Standard:

1a. Students individually and in groups create characters, environments, and actions that create tension and suspense.

1b. Students refine and record dialogue and action.

Content Standard 2

Acting by developing basic acting skills to portray characters who interact in improvised and scripted scenes.

Achievement Standard:

2a. Students analyze descriptions, dialogue, and actions to discover, articulate, and justify character motivation and invent character behaviors based on the observation of interactions, ethical choices, and emotional responses of people.

2b. Students demonstrate acting skills such as sensory recall, concentration, breath control, diction, body alignment, and control of isolated body parts to develop characterizations that suggest artistic choices.

2c. Students in an ensemble interact as the invented characters.

Content Standard 3

Designing by developing environments for improvised and scripted scenes.

Achievement Standard:

3a. Students explain the functions and interrelated nature of scenery, properties, lighting, sound, costumes, and makeup in creating an environment appropriate for the drama.

3b. Students analyze improvised and scripted scenes for technical requirements.

3c. Students develop focused ideas for the environment using visual elements (line, texture, color, space), visual principles (repetition, balance, emphasis, contrast, unity), and aural qualities (pitch, rhythm, dynamics, tempo, expression) from traditional and nontraditional sources.

3d. Students work collaboratively and safely to select and create elements of scenery, properties, lighting, and sound to signify environments, costumes, and makeup to suggest character.

Content Standard 4

Directing by organizing rehearsals for improvised and scripted scenes.

Achievement Standard:

4a. Students lead small groups in planning visual and aural elements and in rehearsing improvised and scripted scenes, demonstrating social, group, and consensus skills.

Content Standard 5

Researching by using cultural and historical information to support improvised and scripted scenes.

Achievement Standard:

5a. Students apply research from print and non-print sources to script writing, acting, design, and directing choices.

Content Standard 6

Comparing and incorporating art forms by analyzing methods of presentation and audience response for theatre, dramatic media (such as film, television, and electronic media), and other art forms.

Achievement Standard:

6a. Students describe characteristics and compare the presentation of characters, environments, and actions in theatre, musical theatre, dramatic media, dance, and visual arts.

6b. Students incorporate elements of dance, music, and visual arts to express ideas and emotions in improvised and scripted scenes.

6c. Students express and compare personal reactions to several art forms.

6d. Students describe and compare the functions and interaction of performing and visual artists and audience members in theatre, dramatic media, musical theatre, dance, music, and visual arts.

Content Standard 7

Analyzing, evaluating, and constructing meanings from improvised and scripted scenes and from theatre, film, television, and electronic media productions.

Achievement Standard:

7a. Students describe and analyze the effect of publicity, study guides, programs, and physical environments on audience response and appreciation of dramatic performances.

7b. Students articulate and support the meanings constructed from their and others' dramatic performances.

7c. Students use articulated criteria to describe, analyze, and constructively evaluate the perceived effectiveness of artistic choices found in dramatic performances.

7d. Students describe and evaluate the perceived effectiveness of students' contributions to the collaborative process of developing improvised and scripted scenes.

Content Standard 8

Understanding context by analyzing the role of theatre, film, television, and electronic media in the community and in other cultures.

Achievement Standard:

8a. Students describe and compare universal characters and situations in dramas from and about various cultures and historical periods, illustrate in improvised and scripted scenes, and discuss how theatre reflects a culture.

8b. Students explain the knowledge, skills, and discipline needed to pursue careers and avocational opportunities in theatre, film, television, and electronic media.

8c. Students analyze the emotional and social impact of dramatic events in their lives, in the community, and in other cultures.

8d. Students explain how culture affects the content and production values of dramatic performances.

8e. Students explain how social concepts such as cooperation, communication, collaboration, consensus, self-esteem, risk taking, sympathy, and empathy apply in theatre and daily life.

Warm-Up Standards

Game	Page	Write		Act			Direct	Analyze			Understand			
		1a. Create	1b. Refine and record	2a. Analyze and invent	2b. Acting skills	2c. Interact	4a. Group skills	7b. Support	7c. Criteria	7d. Evaluate	8a. Compare	8c. Dramatic events	8d. Culture	8e. Interpersonal skills
Adverb Game	11	●		●		●		●	●	●				
And the Winner Is…	44	●		●		●	●	●	●	●				●
Archaeology Game	14	●		●		●	●	●	●	●	●		●	●
A Touch of …	50	●		●	●	●		●	●	●				
Backpack Game	36	●	●	●		●	●	●	●	●				●
Brand Name Game	19	●		●		●	●	●	●	●				●
Don't Do That!	21	●		●		●	●	●	●	●				●
Hobbies	30	●		●		●		●	●	●				
I've Got the Message	40	●		●	●	●	●	●	●	●				●
Let the Games Begin	38	●		●	●	●	●	●	●	●				●
Museum of Oddities	23	●		●		●	●	●	●	●				●
Musical Comedy	46	●	●	●	●	●	●	●	●	●	●		●	●
My Pet Boa	48	●		●		●		●	●	●				●
Preposition Game	42	●	●	●	●	●	●	●	●	●				●
Saying Hello	28	●		●		●	●	●	●	●	●	●	●	●
Tableaux (Frozen Pictures)	34	●		●		●	●	●	●	●	●	●	●	
Useful Utensils	52	●		●		●		●	●	●				●
We're Going on a Vacation	32	●		●		●		●	●	●				●
Who Invited You?	16	●		●		●	●	●	●	●				●
Why Can't I?	54	●		●		●	●	●	●	●				●
You Got Me What?	26	●		●		●	●	●	●	●				●

Characterization Standards

Game	Page	Write		Act			Direct	Analyze			Understand			
		1a. Create	1b. Refine and record	2a. Analyze and invent	2b. Acting skills	2c. Interact	4a. Group skills	7b. Support	7c. Criteria	7d. Evaluate	8a. Compare	8c. Dramatic events	8d. Culture	8e. Interpersonal skills
Clothes Make the Person	65	●		●		●	●	●	●	●	●		●	●
Color Me Pink	68	●	●	●		●	●	●	●	●				●
Devil Made Me Do It	95	●	●	●		●	●	●	●	●				●
Faculty Meeting	59	●		●		●	●	●	●	●				●
Friends Forever	70	●		●		●	●	●	●	●				●
High Five!	72	●		●		●	●	●	●	●			●	●
I'm an Ox!	63	●		●		●	●	●	●	●	●		●	●
In the Mood	78	●		●		●	●	●	●	●				●
It's My Name!	91	●		●		●	●	●	●	●				●
Job Interview	93	●		●		●	●	●	●	●				●
My Tiara	74	●	●	●		●	●	●	●	●				●
Phobia Game	80	●		●		●	●	●	●	●				●
Please and Thank You	76	●		●		●	●	●	●	●				●
Relationship Dyads	84	●		●		●	●	●	●	●				●
Skillful	86	●		●		●	●	●	●	●				●
Trapped with a Libra	99	●		●		●	●	●	●	●	●		●	●
Valley Girls vs. Snobs	89	●		●		●	●	●	●	●	●		●	●
Virtuous Family	97	●		●		●	●	●	●	●	●		●	●
What's Wrong with Me?	61	●		●		●	●	●	●	●				●

Narrative/Plot Standards

Game	Page	Write 1a. Create	1b. Refine and record	Act 2a. Analyze and invent	2b. Acting skills	2c. Interact	Direct 4a. Group skills	Analyze 7b. Support	7c. Criteria	7d. Evaluate	Understand 8a. Compare	8c. Dramatic events	8d. Culture	8e. Interpersonal skills
Big Moment, The	105	●	●	●		●	●	●	●	●		●		●
Bird in the Hand, A	132	●		●		●	●	●	●	●	●	●	●	●
Birth of the Blobs, The	126	●		●		●	●	●	●	●				●
Glimpses	116	●		●	●	●	●	●	●	●				●
In the Lounge	138	●		●		●	●	●		●	●	●	●	●
In the Manner Of ...	120	●		●	●	●	●	●	●	●		●	●	●
It Happened Here	122	●		●	●	●	●	●	●	●				●
It's a Mystery	107	●	●	●		●	●	●	●	●				●
It's Your Lucky Day!	118	●	●	●		●	●	●	●	●				●
Last Chance Saloon	150	●		●		●	●	●	●	●				●
Lima Beans	114	●		●	●	●	●	●	●	●		●	●	●
Magic Shop	144	●		●		●	●	●	●	●	●			●
Our House	110	●	●	●	●	●	●	●	●	●	●	●	●	●
Our Trip to Rio	152	●	●	●		●	●	●	●	●				●
Read All about It	140	●		●	●	●	●	●	●	●	●	●	●	●
Real Estate Agent	112	●		●	●	●	●	●	●	●	●	●	●	●
Resolutions	130	●		●		●	●	●	●	●		●		●
Rituals	136	●	●	●		●	●	●	●	●	●	●	●	●
Sherlock Holmes	103	●	●	●		●	●	●	●	●				●
Super Powers	146	●		●		●	●	●	●	●	●			●
Two Thumbs Up!	128	●	●	●	●	●	●	●	●	●			●	●
What If?	148	●		●		●	●	●	●	●	●			●

Resources

Abbott, John. *The Improvisation Book*. Nick Hern Books, 2007.

Belt, Lynda. *Improv Game Book II*. Thespis Productions, 1994.

Belt, Lynda and Rebecca Stockley. *Improvisations Through Theatre Sports*. Thespis Productions, 1991.

Bernardi, Philip. *Improvisation Starters*. Betterway Books, 1992.

Boal, Augusto. *Games for Actors and Non-actors*. Routledge, 2002.

Book, Stephen. *Improvisation Technique for the Professional Actor in Film, Theatre, and Television*. Silman-James Press, 2002.

Caltagirone, Dennis. *Theatre Arts, The Dynamics of Acting*. Fourth Edition. National Textbook Company, 1996.

Cassady, Marsh. *Acting Games*. Meriwether Publishing Ltd., 1993.

Cassady, Marsh. *Spontaneous Performance*. Meriwether Publishing Ltd., 2000.

Caruso, Sandra and Susan Kosoff. *The Young Actor's Book of Improvisation*. Heinemann, 1998.

Diggles, Dan. *Improv for Actors*. Allworth Press, 2004.

Edelstein, Linda N. *Writer's Guide to Character Traits*. Writers Digest Books, 1999.

Emunah, Renée. *Acting for Real*. Bruner-Routledge, 1994.

Foreman, Kathleen Joyce and Clem Martini. *Something Like a Drug*. Red Deer College Press, 1995.

Frager, Robert, ed. *Who Am I?* Penguin Group (USA) Inc., 1994.

Hall, William and Paul Killam, ed. *The San Francisco Bay Area Theatresports Playbook, Edition 5.3*. Bay Area Theatresports, 1998.

Halpern, Charna. *Truth in Comedy*. Meriwether Publishing Ltd., 1994.

Hazenfield, Carol. *Acting on Impulse*. Coventry Creek Press, 2002.

Heimburg, Jason and Justin Heimburg. *The Official Movie Plot Generator*. Publishers Group West, 2004.

Horn, Delton T. *Comedy Improvisation*. Meriwether Publishing Ltd., 1991.

Johnston, Chris. *House of Games*. Psychology Press, 1998.

Johnstone, Keith. *Impro*. Routledge, 2012.

Johnstone, Keith. *Impro for Storytellers*. Routledge/Theatre Arts Books, 1999.

Jones, Justine and Mary Ann Kelley. *Drama Games and Improvs*. Meriwether Publishing Ltd., 2007.

Jones, Justine and Mary Ann Kelley. *Improv Ideas*. Meriwether Publishing Ltd., 2006.

Jones, Justine and Mary Ann Kelley. *Staging an Interactive Mystery Play*. Meriwether Publishing Ltd., 2012.

Keirsey, David. *Please Understand Me II*. Prometheus Nemesis, 1998.

Koppett, Kat. *Training to Imagine*. Stylus Publishing, LLC., 2001.

Lynn, Bill. *Improvisation for Actors and Writers*. Meriwether Publishing Ltd., 2004.

Novelly, Maria. *Theatre Games for Young Performers*. Meriwether Publishing Ltd., 1985.

O'Neill, Cecily. *Drama Guidelines*. Heinemann Educational Books in association with London Drama, 1977.

Pollock, Michael and Jason Alexander. *Musical Improv Comedy.* Masteryear Publishing, 2004.

Salinsky, Tom and Deborah Frances-White. *The Improv Handbook.* Bloomsbury Methuen Drama, 2008.

Seham, Amy E. *Whose Improv Is It Anyway?* University Press of Mississippi, 2001.

Scher, Anna and Charles Verrall. *Another 100+ Ideas for Drama.* Heinemann Educational Books, 1987.

Schmidt, Victoria Lynn. *45 Master Characters.* Writers Digest Books, 2007.

Schnupp, Alvin J. *Bravo!* Meriwether Publishing Ltd., 2001.

Spolin, Viola. *Improvisation for the Theatre.* Third Edition. Northwestern University Press, 1999.

Spolin, Viola. *Theatre Games for Rehearsal.* Northwestern University Press, 1985.

Spolin, Viola. *Theatre Games for the Classroom.* Northwestern University Press, 1986.

Sternberg, Patricia and Lisa A. Barnett. *Theatre for Conflict Resolution.* Heinemann Educational Books, 1998.

Zimmerman, Suzi. *More Theatre Games for Young Performers.* Meriwether Publishing Ltd., 2004.

About the Authors

Since moving to the U.K. in 2005, **Justine Jones** has thrown herself into courses in improv, drama therapy, socio-drama, and psychodrama, all of which have added to her understanding of the process of making theatre. As well as spending a great deal of time at the theatre, Justine works as a Jungian sand-play therapist with children and adolescents. She is amazed at how extraordinary the stories people tell about their lives really are and thinks that we are all improvising our lives and our life story as we go along. She is currently researching the relationship of story to various forms of therapy and is seeing every day that life really is theatre!

Now retired to a small town in north-central Florida, **Mary Ann Kelley** has time to involve herself in community and theatre activities in the area. Each fall, her small Victorian town of 400 people opens its arms to about 40,000 visitors for its 1890s Festival, complete with craft booths lining the oak-canopied streets. Mary Ann's part in the festival includes editing a tabloid newspaper full of stories about the town's history and current doings. She also finds time to be active in her local garden club and yoga group. She credits her friends, and her yoga teachers and group, with helping her get the most out of life. Her most recent design and painting efforts have not been on-stage, but rather in her 1891 farmhouse.

Order Form

Meriwether Publishing Ltd.
PO Box 7710
Colorado Springs CO 80933-7710
Phone: 800-937-5297 Fax: 719-594-9916
Website: www.meriwether.com

Please send me the following books:

_____ **Improv Ideas 2 #BK-B356**   **$22.95**
by Justine Jones and Mary Ann Kelley
A new book of games and lists for the classroom and beyond

_____ **Improv Ideas #BK-B283**   **$24.95**
by Justine Jones and Mary Ann Kelley
A book of games and lists

_____ **Drama Games and Improvs #BK-B296**   **$22.95**
by Justine Jones and Mary Ann Kelley
Games for the classroom and beyond

_____ **Drama Games and Acting Exercises #BK-B311** **$17.95**
by Rod Martin
177 games and activities

_____ **Group Improvisation #BK-B259**   **$16.95**
by Peter Gwinn with additional material by Charna Halpern
The manual of ensemble improv games

_____ **112 Acting Games #BK-B277**   **$19.95**
by Gavin Levy
A comprehensive workbook of theatre games

_____ **275 Acting Games: Connected #BK-B314**   **$19.95**
by Gavin Levy
A comprehensive workbook of theatre games for developing acting skills

These and other fine Meriwether Publishing books are available at your local bookstore or direct from the publisher. Prices subject to change without notice. Check our website or call for current prices.

Name: _____ e-mail: _____

Organization name: _____

Address: _____

City: _____ State: _____

Zip: _____ Phone: _____

❑ **Check enclosed**
❑ **Visa / MasterCard / Discover / Am. Express #** _____

Signature: _____   *Expiration date:* _____ / _____   *CVV code:* _____
(required for credit card orders)

Colorado residents: Please add 3% sales tax.
Shipping: Include $3.95 for the first book and 75¢ for each additional book ordered.

❑ *Please send me a copy of your complete catalog of books and plays.*